Dorothy Poetry
Emotional Healing
thru
Christ

Dorothy Poetry
Emotional Healing
thru Christ

DOROTHY F WILLIAMS ALSTON

authorHOUSE®

AuthorHouse™
1663 Liberty Drive
Bloomington, IN 47403
www.authorhouse.com
Phone: 1-800-839-8640

Published by AuthorHouse   04/16/2013

ISBN: 978-1-4634-0904-3 (sc)
ISBN: 978-1-4634-0909-8 (hc)
ISBN: 978-1-4634-0907-4 (e)

Library of Congress Control Number: 2013905572

Any people depicted in stock imagery provided by Thinkstock are models, and such images are being used for illustrative purposes only.
Certain stock imagery © Thinkstock.

This book is printed on acid-free paper.

Because of the dynamic nature of the Internet, any web addresses or links contained in this book may have changed since publication and may no longer be valid. The views expressed in this work are solely those of the author and do not necessarily reflect the views of the publisher, and the publisher hereby disclaims any responsibility for them.

INTRODUCTION

And Jesus looking upon them saith, With men it is impossible, but not with God: for with God all things are possible.—Mark 10:27 (King James Version)

I am a fifty-seven-year old African American woman. I was born and raised in a small town in North Carolina. My life was like ancient, rundown furniture that no one wanted. I haven't had an easy life by any means. I have faced many obstacles that I sincerely thought I was born to suffer. Does the Lord love me? What did I do to have so many stumbling blocks thrown my way? Why did an evil spirit want me as a child? I believe the abuse I suffered at the secret mind and body of elders' women and men played a big part in this.

The love of my mother (Omega) and sister (M) and my two brothers—Williams, Haywood, Alston, my baptism members, and West End will always be limitless, and this book will attest to that. I never knew my real father, but my stepfather, John Haywood and his niece Clara Haywood, greatly helped me!

But I've experienced anguish I thought only existed beyond this life. All I wanted was love from an honest community West End and kinfolks. I fell in love with a man who was fifteen years older than me. I was seventeen, and my mother warned me he was married. After that I became pregnant.

My mother, Omega, and sister, raised my daughter Tasha Williams until she was five. I moved to North Carolina and moved in a gang with a married man who was eleven years older. I suppose it was considered an unsafe home life.

In 1981 I became a nurse's aid, which was a miracle—now I had income. I lost a good job at a main nursing facility because of my man's jealousy. He always wanted me to take the conflicting opinion of "menfolk" over my own. I believe a real man backs up a positive viewpoint! I was distressed and weary about the lack of nursing assistance jobs in North Carolina. In addition, my man was beating me in the streets, in other people's houses, everywhere! And it took

1

several years to get away. When there is no love at home, it is time to go so my sister raised Tasha!

Over the period of about fifteen years I suffered a lot of emotional abuse, mental anguish, and physical abuse. I lost numerous jobs. I was shot in the face, I was pistol whipped, and the man was enraged enough to try to kill me by driving my vehicle over an embankment. Then an acquaintance tried to rape me but I defended myself by cutting him with a dagger and stabbing him. The list goes on. Then I moved to Oxford, North Carolina, until I met Lonnie and left the North Carolina in January 1985, where I moved to New Jersey and got married 1986 in North Carolina.

God sent me Lonnie M. Alston, and he was a really stand-up guy. I became pregnant and named my son Lonnie K. Alston. Shortly after I gave birth to Brittny C. Alston.

We were restoring our lives together with my daughter Tasha. We were a real family. I saw Tasha and other kinfolk all the time.

In 1989 I got as job as a nurse's aid at a well-known rehabilitation home in New Jersey. Later I was working at the Elizabeth CA Rehabilitation Home and the Rahway Hospital when one day while working at the hospital I had an accident and bruised my back. That injury took me out of work.

In 1991, I had automobile accident that further damaged a nerve root in my back. This accident resulted in my having nerve damage and a mini stroke, and I was unable to walk well. The doctor relayed to me that I would have about a 30 percent chance of walking for the rest of my life.

After I was married I moved therapy at a medical center there. I received that treatment for five years. During that time a doctor found a hole in my back caused by a bone disease, and 2005 I had to have six screws placed in my back. Two of the screws broke during the operation (which the doctor took no responsibility for), causing me to have my first stroke. Instead of repairing the damage, he caused more damage to me. I was unable to walk, and I didn't even know the screws were broken in my back. I went through three months of rehab in a nursing facility. In 2006 I received another operation to repair the damage and had a second stroke on the operating table. This stroke left me unable to speak or write. At the time I couldn't walk or write. I became extremely terrified and furious with the doctors! *Please, God,* I prayed, *send me one angel to help me and I will turn faith to you.*

I stopped believing in man's words, which had always left me shattered. What did I do? I don't remember anything!

I love my mother (Omega) and sister (M) (thank you both!), who transferred me back to my hometown to continue rehab for several more months. Upon my release I had nurses work with me in my home. At this time I had gained a large amount of weight (I weighed 289 pounds). The doctors said I needed to take twenty-five pills a day, but I was sick of pills, so I tossed them. I became a diabetic taking insulin shots.

At this point my faith took a greater leap. I was determined to trust, to be optimistic about my recovery and to walk, have awareness, and talk again. I worked hard to have faith in the report of the lord. There were struggles in the midst of my victory. I was hard-pressed to believe God's word, which said by his stripes I am healed (Isaiah 53:5).

Once people read my stories and poetry, they will know I am a miracle. I am alive for a purpose, and that is to testify to those who are lost so they can receive hope, can trust again. "When life gives you lemons," as someone has sort of said, "you make a bad-ass lemonade, determined to find a connection with God!" My life has had many ups and downs.

My obstacles include life as a former gang member and yes! Sugar Daddy R. played a major role in my gang life. He exposed me to big money, gambling and guns. Several times, in 25 years he almost pushed me to kill him. Later I even went to jail several time because of stealing for the intention to help the people in my community, but God was always with me. I was a possessions prostitute whore or wage for sex, dealing with painkillers, alcoholic drink, bone disease, several strokes, loss of jobs, and a husband who left me in January 2000. At the time I could walk or write.

After my car accident I attempted suicide because my husband said good-bye, so I became a psychiatric inpatient in June 2001.

It made me realize I needed to tell my story. I wanted to let others know that no matter what you face, you have to press on and believe first in God and then yourself. This is my journey within and the empowerment I received by denouncing man and exalting God.

Seven years have passed since making that decision. It is now 2013; I am still under a doctor's care and am in constant pain. I sought another doctor to see if another surgery could correct the broken screws, but he informed me that another surgery was out of the question. He said I would not survive the lengthy hours under anesthesia. This doctor also informed me that the first surgery was unnecessary and had been done experimentally. The only way to resolve this legal matter is to hire an attorney. I have spoken with one, and he indicated it would be impossible to win because I am in a better shape now than I was then and at least now I'm walking.

My question is, where is the justice for people like me? This is why I have to trust God for my total 100 percent healing. The Lord willing, he has a special prayer to help me assist my children and grandchildren and transport them to truth and unadulterated faith in God!

Hebrews 10:36 says, "For ye have need of patience, that, after ye have done the will of God, ye might receive the promise" (KJV).

Thank you Lord—and his name is Jesus—inner self strength lives within us all.

DEDICATION TO MY MOTHER

Evangelist Omega Amanda Williams was a strong Christian woman who really loved the Lord. Mom raised two daughters (Dorothy and her sister), John and 1 son, grandchildren, and great-grandchildren. I wanted you to remember who this woman praised. She was religious at the altar and in churches and other places of worship, and she really loved playing her spiritual organ at home. Whenever you saw her, she daily walked always carried a Bible. Mom at all times spoke a religious word about God and communicated with the Lord in her home. Mom loved caroling, gospel choir music, and she danced to praised. Mom was well-known. She was courageous and spoke in public. Mom branched out and touched many others in different churches. Mom wore robes to church on Sundays and always carried a Bible. Her strong faith helped me learn how to trust the Lord and get on with my emotional healing. Mom would take me to visit elders' houses, where they helped people with healings, prayer, and preaching. Mom love Bible school meetings and loved Sundays and Gospel programs. My mother's relationship with Christ was beautiful.

Mom's body is gone but she is at spiritual peace with the Lord. I know why God called her home! Her torch here will continue to be carried for long time.

We live everlastingly life, loving Christ as Mom did, so we have joyfulness. My mom testified truth, and it helped me have faith, even during her sickness until the end. Every day I sob because I didn't comprehend not hearing her voice or her playing her organ. I know my faithlessness is healing, it has moved out. I join together with the world where Mom made it positive and believed in paradise every day! Powerful prayer aims the virtuous word toward us that God communicates is alive!

Revelation 21:24 says, "And the nation of them which are saved shall walk in the light of it: and the kings of the earth do bring their glory and honors into it" (KJV).

"Evangelist Omega Amanda Williams
ALPHA OMEGA
APRIL 4, 1930 to FEBRUARY 4, 2011 11:00
Elmwood Cemetery, North Carolina
THE Holy Bible
Evangelist Omega A. Williams, 2009
**The Battle Is God for the True Trinity Holiness
Church of God"**

 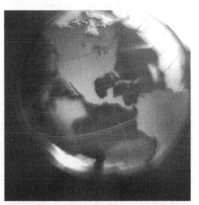

People, don't you try to fight the battle, let God fight for you. You'll be glad you did. You will see yourself growing in God's grace and love, and you will not fret yourself over evildoing but delight yourself in God. He will work it out for you. I want to be greater for God on this earth and appreciate what he has done for our family and other families.

There has been time I didn't have shoes on my feet; I had no clothes and no food. I am so glad God loves me. Dear God, please touch your little children for me right now. I will overcome my enemy as will you. God has given me a great job—he had made me. Dear God, please touch your little children for me right now. I saw the Spirit of the Lord upon me. That is why I know God put me here at the True Trinity Holiness Church—called by God and found by God and me. I am so glad God loves me. I am still praising God for all the things he has given me, for all he has done for me and the family he gave me. He gave us Holy life, and no man can take from God and us. He'll do the same for you. Why not come right now from where you are living? God wants you saved, and so do I.

I saw a new heaven and a new earth—no other God before him. The good and the bad—oh, give thank unto the Lord; his mercy endures forever! Believe that God is God and he gave his life for us to be saved, and believe there is a heaven and hell. It is good for us to be here in the name of Jesus.

"And I saw a new heaven and a new earth: for the first heaven and the first earth were passed away; and there was no more sea" (Revelations 21:1, KJV).

Mama's Homecoming Is in the Clouds

Evangelist Omega Amanda Williams

It is impossible to call Mama. Sorry! Mama, you left in a hurry, without us once again saying thanks: thanks for religious compassion when we worried, thanks for religious encouraging words when we were lonely. Thanks for religious favor when we were discouraged, thanks for religious provisions when we hungry, thanks for enlightening us with religious songs that show God cares. If we had a thousand tongues we could not thank you enough. But the road leads to golden angels in the clouds, a seventh heaven with your grace.

And mercy won the race. "Mama, yes!" The roads were rough, filled at times with weakness, pain, bills, and debts, and the jobs got tougher, until your faith one day brought you to see your Bible.

When you stumble upon God's Holy face, I hope in the future, Mama, to see your face in the clouds. Mama, homecoming *is* your reward. I see both hands and angel wings waving with that smile."

Our original family hope to connect my sister and brothers Williams, Haywood, and Alston, as well as relatives and friends in fellowship who will always testify to God.

"Our families, team spirit, and friends thank you for all endeavors of benevolence revealed during prays for Mom. May God endure to bless us. We express gratitude (special recognitions) to our Baptist Church family in addition: Natalie Watkins, Rehabilitation and Healthcare.

I am still grieved over the loss of Mother because she was waiting for this book every day! May God surely bless you and thank you for your patience; forgive and forget and support my manuscript! Thank you.

—DFWA, February 4, 2011

"Therefore you now have sorrow; but I will see you again and your heart will rejoice, and your joy no one will take from you" (John 16:22, KJV).

I will see God truly and then affirm to see him and Mom in heaven. I've grieved and communicate to be heard.

Today, Mom and Williams, Haywood, and Alston have moved on to heaven. Our family faced rough, uneven roads: illness, work afflictions, bills, and tough jobs. The news release states, "Goodness was your families, and God's holy smile can be seen on their faces. Their spirituality tasted sweet honey and feasted at God's banquet tables. I know God wants us glorious, gratifying, and peaceful together. We don't understand when God has plans for us and then man tries to tell us what happened. Surely one day we may take a leave of absence to spend time with heavenly Father.

People will see God is alive. My family waits now to share testimony. All families are not utterly alone. The virtuous news is for all families who wait for the everlasting. In Isaiah 26:3, God said,

"Thou wilt keep him in perfect peace, whose mind is stayed on thee: because he trusteth in thee" (KJV).

We will hopefully someday see faces in the clouds, with two golden chariots ridden by spirits and pulled by white horses. Our departed family may say, "Mother, aunts, cousins, uncles, grandparents, and other loved ones, everyday we love you in our hearts."

I believe joy comes in the morning, forgoing our family held in "standby" for our heavenly Father. I now understand heartily that it's believable Mom is gone. All family is alive. Faith the size of a mustard seed means it's possible to endure the hardships and make a straight road aimed toward peace in heaven. God is everlasting for all families and friends. We can put God first to connection; the prize is truly long-lasting, wonderful, joyful, and peaceful.

> "And God will wipe away every tear from their eyes; there shall be no more death, nor sorrow, nor crying. There shall be no more pains, for the former things have passed away" (Revelation 21:4, New King James Version).

God's Love satisfies us in the never-ending. I remember Mom died . . . endless dampness in those tears. Now God has been kindhearted and dried Dorothy's tears.

—DFWA February 11, 2011

A M B RECORDZ abmkane2007@aol.com (KANE) this is my only son ***LONNIE K. ALSTON and all beat/Christmas is his music***

"I can do all things through Christ which strengtheneth me" (Philippians 4:13, KJV).

I am Dorothy F. W. Alston, who created "Dorothy's God Said, 'I Am Somebody.'" I found strength of mind to believe with help from God. I surely will create my melody tracks at the top of the list!

"And there came a voice out of the cloud, saying, 'This is my beloved Son: hear him'" (Luke 9:35, KJV).

"God said, 'Dorothy, you are somebody'"

I'm not a voice who speaks no spirituals words. Nor at times did I hear carelessly good words seeking to discover who Dorothy is. Some people still called this name "sock it to me," so I took to the streets, a prostitute lustfully running with evil men gangs. At this time I was badly behaved and had quite an attitude.

I sought men for their attractiveness, love, and wealth. I asked questions: "Why does God or anybody care?"

The sky said in a humble, sweet voice, "Yes, Dorothy, somebody here loves you, sweet child. Let no man deprive you of God or your pride."

Rewards come from God; prizes are eternal. Yes, do all things in your heart.

When Flossy (that's me) had no shoes or socks to wear, the Lord gave me sandals and garments.

People who said, "Flossy, you were nothing but a liar" didn't even give me a piece of bread, never mind balm the negatives. I am a drug addict who wants to get high and forget your name. Flossy asked my neighborhoods and said nothing. And certain friends what happen about I have your back?" I think they were scared why didn't help me?

God took away the drugs and showed me a path toward new heights. Now, joy is a sunrise everyday to praise the Lord. In my mind's eye I clearly see the positives: "Dorothy, you are somebody" cleaned this one soul, and as a result I help families and communities. Now joy is a sunrise everyday.

My homeboys and I were intoxicated, sat on blocks, in vacated cars, walked with it each day. Yes, Flossy lived in condemned houses and slept around ordinary fighting, remedies, party houses, anywhere I could on the W. E. corners.

Flossy risked high bets against nightly spiritual evil, where we traded bargains. Flossy took care of these needs and then kneeled. So-called Baptist churchgoers silently mocked: "Who's that whore?" Schoolmates' nickname for me was "Sock It To Me."

I was a scholar who wanted an education. Some teacher who stood at the front row would say, "Dorothy cannot comprehend." My grades were low, but I was bold and mad and at an age where they thought I was perhaps "slow." Something teachers don't dare call ("Error!") children anymore.

So I made people laugh and made them smile, involved them, demanded they help.

Then an elderly man put me in manacles! I loved him! He introduced me to a new world. I made so many changes, but it was time to go. A past man was using his power of a gun, to try to kill me. Then why did husband separated? Was it love? Certainly not money, and yes, maybe he had another woman. I wondered, was I mistaken? Am I somebody?

Yes, "holy" Baptist church-gossips, your sisters and brothers, who are a creation of God, are human beings. I abhorred men and didn't like what I saw in the mirror. So I tried killing self-loathing and willed myself over and over: Please help with the waterworks! Lord, will you please have faith in me to help?

The awaiting aristocrat dried tears, took away all drugs, shivers, secretions, and horrific tastes.

"Truly I know it is so, but how can a man be righteous before God?" (Job 9:2, NKJV).

Psalm 142:5: "I cried unto thee, O LORD: I said, 'Thou art my refuge and my portion in the land of the living" (NKJV). God knows and sees Dorothy in all works because deep down she was searching her soul from the pit of hell.

Some people thought I would never make it, until God touched and converted passion to this one mortal. He asked, "Who are you?" I said, "It is me, Dorothy F. W. Alston."

"God said, 'And now abide faith, hope, love, these three; but the greatest of these is love'" (1 Corinthians 13:13, NKJV).

"Dorothy," God said, "you are somebody." I was still alive, reflecting, certainly no longer going astray.

"Bless the Lord O my soul: all that is within me bless his holy name!" (Psalm 103:1, NKJV).

I personally believe in life, guidance, and good fortune to move ahead. Thank you, Lord, who listens and loves. You are living truth. Always confidently praise the Lord.

The Lord sends help, and he moves us to a higher level. Yes, Dorothy's victory is to be believed. Lord, you are real, and we recognize the truth!

To Dorothy Faye Williams Alston, God said, "You are somebody."

—D. F. W. A. (Sock It To Me/Flossy), February 2, 2000

Looking Back over My Life

Tribute: Birthday Celebration

Emotional Healing Through

RSVP: 21 & OVER

Admission: $10.00 Tickets: $10.00 (Brenda B, Neal, Liz Hart, And Mary G. Ricks)

NO WEAPONS OR FIREARMS/There will be security.

Never Would Have Made It

Tiffany's of Henderson 110 South Garnett Street October 2, 2010 7:00n to 9:00

Birthday & Tribute to: "Dorothy's Poetry/Emotional Healing through Christ," the spirited working of a hardback-evident Black Woman Looking Back over My Life

Videographer   : Ray Green

Instrumental Gospel   Music Tony Finch

Introduction by   Tasha Williams

Daughter of Rising Artist

Gospel Song: "I Believe" by Cecelia Alston

Introduction by Brittny Alston

Poetry: "I AM Somebody" by Dorothy Faye Williams Alston

Movie: "Christmas Miracles for the Homeless"

Blessing by Alfreda Mcknight

Dinner serving staff: Faye Jordan, Lizzie Hart, Mary G. Ricks, Brenda B. Neal, and Zelwaureco A. Hill

"Gorial A. Hill sent a large donation to Dorothy"

Entertainment: Cecelia Alston

Two songs: "I Am Nobody" and "Still Here"

Attire: Dress Casual (no sneakers, hats, jeans, etc., but dress comfortably)

No brown bagging permitted.

No weapons or firearms! There will be security John Haywood Jr, Tony Finch

Thank you to Mary A. Jones, Glady Bethea, Jame Harris, etc.

D. F. W. Alston, October 2, 2010

Hi. My name is Dorothy Alston. God doesn't care who you are or what you look like. I can do altogether anything while working toward God's kingdom! In life sometimes, I was negative because from my past to the present, I felt worthless. I thought nobody wanted to love me, but I am here to tell you there is someone who loves me for who I am. I was lost in the broken-up space of my tiny lifecycle: Baptist churches, family, friends, and a husband, and I thought nobody loved me. I used to think and believe I couldn't do anything right and would use foul language with everyone. I was unhappy over the slow road in life, and I told Satan, "This isn't your mind or body!"

I said to God, "Made me a fisherman."

"Now, Dorothy, there is one God who understands," God told me. He loves me and the whole world. He is a God who rises to relationships, hope, trusting, learning, forgiving, and forgetting, and he loves to come into my life. His name is Jesus.

"For whoever shall keep whole law, and yet stumble in one point, he is guilty of all" (James 2:10, NKJV).

His name is Lord and Savior Jesus Christ. On December 10, 2000, I had night visions. God appeared, and a sweet, soft voice said, "Dorothy F. W. Alston, you are somebody."

I have written spiritual poems and a spiritual story over the years and never did I feel I had accomplished what I wanted with these poems. Then one night God told me to draw a clear vision. The next morning I began to structure a play, "Christmas Miracles for the Homeless." God gave me spiritual positive thinking in order to write that play.

I had rough and severely emotional responsibilities in life. The invitations said, "I'm inviting you to join me to watch a 'spiritual play' called 'Christmas Miracles for the Homeless,' and see what happens to people when we forget who Jesus is. I can testify that bad things happened to me in life; nevertheless, the help of God, characters, and Baptist members helped me through it. Currently, I am writing spiritual poems and creating cards using the talents God has blessed me with.

"The play will take place on December 22, 2001, at 6:00 p.m. at Vance Granville Community College Civic Center, US 158 in Henderson, North Carolina.

"I am a living witness that God doesn't care what we are, that God can use anybody to do his work."

I created a club on October 17, 2001, called "The Children's Wish List." I prayed, with the help of the homeless, that this club would be successful in years to come. If you would like a ticket, the contribution is $7.00. If you would like to donate to helping the Children's Wish List, please call (252) 000-0000.

—Dorothy Alston, December 21, 2001

"Dorothy's Christmas Miracles for the Homeless"
a play by D. F. A.
October 3, 2010
(The play was exceedingly entertaining and included
music by my husband, Lonnie M. Alston, and my son
Lonnie Alston.)
First scene
The curtain rises
Sarah P. Murphy

One Corinthians 9:11 says, "If we have sown spiritual things for you, is it a great thing if we reap your material things?"

We are more than blessed to have a rooftop over our heads. All family should provide foods And clothing. Surely you are blessed with currency paid in full edification, everyday jobs, and our child or children living with us. I would like you to focus on people who are less fortunate, who do not have these blessings. There are people who don't care to kill, who aren't too envious to love or to share.

Around us are populaces without food, money, homes, or jobs. If you have never been homeless, can you possibly know what it is like? You can go to bed rich and wake up the next morning with a sign on your door that says "Get out." Everyday someone becomes homeless, or children loses their parents and become part of the underground culture. These homeless people and families survive on railway routes, in strongboxes, or train cars. They become vagrants. When a child runs away and joins up with a gang, those members become his or her family.

I am here to tell you I know a man who stands high and looks low. The Lord does not care what your appearance is like; we will never be judged or found guilty. I want you to know he loves everybody. All we have to do is ask for what you want, and the spirit understands and you will receive it.

Poems by Tasha (Sha) Williams of
Rising-Up Artist

"During the Season"
It's during the season when we're busy shopping and
spreading lots of holiday cheer,
Instead of giving God all of the glory,
We give it to the other and/or the brother man
pulling eight reindeer.
Being unfortunate and homeless is stressful and full of
worries,
For instance—What will we eat? Where will we sleep?
Will there be snow or just flurries?
Regardless of who and where we are,
We all must attain and keep our faith and hope,
Without them it's impossible for anyone to cope.
Life is full of changes, ups and downs, and
expectations that never leave the ground,
With faith you have everything and more only if it's in
Christ that you found.
As people we must not turn our backs on those who
have less than others,
But instead embrace them as they were our own
children, cousins, sisters, or brothers.
Christmas is the time of year when we give to and
feed and or pray for the needy,
Because if it wasn't for Christ we could be hungry,
with our stomachs bulging and our eyes glossy and
beady
revised 01/028/02

Special thanks to my husband, Lonnie M. Alston, for the stage lights and Christmas music and to my son, Lonnie K. Alston!

"Dorothy's Christmas Miracles for the Homeless."

Cast of Characters

Narrator Sarah P. Murphy
Dorothy F. W. "Flossy" Alston
Lonnie K., a boy
Brittny Alston
Tasha "Sha" Williams (an adult homeless woman with three homeless children: daughter Shamere and boys Jamario and Michael)
Shamere Haskins
Michael Haskins
Jamario Vass
Joseph Peace
Cassandra Mcburroug (a nurse)
John Haywood Jr.
Marie "First Lady" Jones
Jelise Hart
Adrian Davis
George Vass
Dorothy Mitchell
Brenda B. Neal
Leland Neal
James Edwin Vass
Florence Cheek Vass
Edwin M. Vass
Zelwaureco A. Hill, teenage girl
Frank Bullock
Pastor John H. Neal Jr.

Enter onstage

Sarah P. Murphy

The play focus on the concept that God can use anybody he choose—including lies, whores, drunks, idols, drug user, or a "nobody." Come with me to the streets and see what happen to people when they forget where they come from.

The first scene is about people who obtained great heights at a job, a home business, and family. These people were mail carriers, nurses, stock brokers, pharmacists, photographers, street gangs, and scholars. They lost everything they own because they forgot to ask God to help magnify, glorify, or praise, but then God gave it to them.

One Corinthians 9:11 says, "If we have sown spiritual things for you, is it a great thing if we reap your material things?"

Two Corinthians 6:10 says, "As sorrowful, yet always rejoicing; as poor, yet making many rich; as having nothing, and *yet* possessing all things."

Curtain opens

FLOSSY and ALSTON are elderly homeless women,
and FRANK is a homeless man. They are sitting on
snow—wet park benches.
SHA, SHAMERE, MICHAEL, JOHN, and
JAMARIO walk onstage.
Sha carries a large box.
Actors are divided into two groups and slowly enter
the stage from opposite sides.
Some people are passing newspapers, coffees,
earphones, and stocks.
Nurses, mail carriers, and photographers dress
professionally.
Alston and Frank approach people begging for money
but aren't paid attention, so they walk with their noses
turned up.

Everybody changes outfits into rags.
Two gang-bangers, BRITTNY and JELISE approach
Frank.

John

Whatever happened to feeding the children? This
is embarrassing! We need go back over W. E. Road.
At least my Kingman will make sure you have
distribution.

Brittny
(To Jelise)

Man, I miss Mom's fried chicken and a warm bed to
relax in!
Man, I'm feeling down. This'll be our last snow-white
Christmas living on the street.
(Brittny and Jelise go over to Michael and hit him.
Frank is looking through the trashcan but doesn't find
any bottles or food)

Frank

Sure would be nice if somebody left a dam corner
in that wine bottle! Time sure is getting hard these
days. Somebody has some money? Man, isn't anybody
leaving me a cold Cobra beer? Or people have change
to drop wine-train these days! I wish I had another
can now, maybe a cold Pepsi or an iced tea?
(Dorothy, Alston, and Frank approach people and beg
for money.
These people cross the stage: a whore, photographer,
mail carrier, nurse, and stock broker.)

Flossy and Frank
(alternate their speech)

Man what's up? Can you let me get a dollar? Can I
get a buck fifty? Can you give a sister or brother some
change? Come here, please! Wait a minute!

Dorothy

Can you buy me a three-dollar drink, or will you have
a whisky on the rocks? Please stop! but they don't care.
They are selfish. What does a drunk have to do to get
a drink around here?

Dorothy
(to Alston)

Hey, look—somebody dropped a piece of half-cooked
chicken wing on the ground! I wish I had a piece of
bread, some pig's feet, and Swiss Miss hot chocolate!
(Alston and Frank walk past to a large trashcan and
we made a fire.)

Dorothy

Save me a taste of that wing, Alston. I'm hungry! You
can't possibly be hungry! Last night Dorothy saw
alston looking those four dogs. Turning over those
two trashcans so Alston throw
The dogs a rock because she wanted the food!

Alston

That was my trashcan they were eating out of.
(Alston looks in the trashcan and at the shabby
blanket. She pulls out worn-out socks and puts them on)

Sure hopes these feet's stay warm!

Sha

(walking onstage with newspaper in her hand. She
puts a large box near their head)
(singing out loud) Extra, extra, read it all about it
on the front page! Another homeless person bites
the dust! Hospital fires another nurse for selling
painkillers.

CASSANDRA
(walks across the stage)

(yells) Hey! Everybody want to get high? Anyone? I'm
your bad girl—hello! Anybody needing some uppers
to rock your world? Alston, I have a few pills for half
price and am willing to share.

Sha

Guess you'll to be sleeping with the roaches—and in
that big box too!

Shamere
(to Cassandra)

Will you be living with us on the streets this
Christmas? I am sure Mom can find a large box for
you to sleep in it.

Michael

(approaches the bench)
Can we share her blankets?

Cassandra

No! I'm not sleeping with the roaches. This Christmas
we'll be enjoying a warm bubble bath and sleeping in
a bed on red satin sheets with two soft pillows at the
Holiday Hotel. We'll drink Crown Royal fine whisky
and eat an extensive meal, I hope!

Michael

(walking back inside his mother's box)
(Shouting) Mom! She's mad!
(Joseph and John come onstage and approach Alston.)

Dorothy
(to Flossy)

(yelling) Hey, Flossy! Isn't that the man we saw last
week with a suit, tie, and a camera?

Frank
(to Joseph)

This is a damn shame. Tell me you went penniless
after giggling you got garbage-dump laughing! Isn't
that a damn disgrace? Not *you,* big dog, with your
own camera.

Flossy

Stop! Leaved that man alone! Out in the park he's
somebody. We don't look down at anyone. We are a
family, and he's homeless too!

John

Hey, brother, what's up? Can you let a poor brother
hold a dollar to get a bottle? I began to tremble
overpoweringly; I need a power knockout! Man, when
I get a job, I am going to pay you.

Joseph

Brother, are you kidding? I don't have my company
anymore! I don't have a damn dime. I lost everything:
wife, children, friends. I live where you live! On the
streets!

John

(approaches Joseph and Frank at the fire) (To Frank)
Man, you need a job! We cannot be bumming for you
too.

Dorothy

We sleep and eat at the same roach motel you do.
(Loud and angry) The street!

Sha

Where everybody come and go as they please! In this
park we don't like a thief. Isn't that right, Cassandra?

Cassandra

Yeah! It is hard to sell from your on brothers!

(Jamario)
(standing, facing the actors)

My mother left me. One morning I woke up and
Mom was gone. I waited a day, but she never came
back. I was nine years old when I hit the streets. I'm
tired of living on the streets.

(Adrian)
(comes onstage)

Man! I had it all: cars, women, companies, banks,
and stocks until I forgot just that quick who gave
it to me. After lost my wife, children, and friends,
everything else vanished, so I remember every single
day now!
(he pulls a bottle out of his pants, and start drinking)

(John)

Man, are you still drinking that night train? Please,
how old does a man have to be before he learns and
becomes a real man?
(Leland and Brenda comes onstage and walk to where
all the men are standing)

Leland
(to Brenda)

My father said a man is not a man if he turns his back
on God. Can you tell me why you turn your back on
that brother instead of helping him?

Adrian
(to John)

I can't help Leland when I need help myself.

John

I'm trying to get myself a beer.

Joseph

I don't know about somebody else's problems!

Alston
(to everybody)

(loudly) Well! God don't turn his back on his people! Matter of fact, tell me did my ex-husband kicked me out of the house. And you tell Flossy why. I tried talking, but he was using foul language!

Lonnie
(to Dorothy)

My mother said, "Man will always walk out on his family," and my father was gone when I was a baby! I saw him with another family! So, whatever, my mother don't know where to live day by day!

Brenda

Where's your mother now, son?
Are you afraid to be out on the streets this late?

Lonnie

No, I am not fearful. Besides,
my mother went to get something to eat! **George**

(lifting a large strongbox)
I saw Lonnie looking in the garbage and eating a
cookie. So I told him to ask and wait until his mother
comes back! I had my carpentry plants until I lost
everything because I didn't have the time for going to
church!

Flossy
(to Sha)

Well! I see I am not the only one who is homeless. At
least I got a job!

Sha

You aren't working tonight?

Flossy

Business on the street is tired, and I'm unhappy.

Sha

What's the deal? Who put those twelve stitches in
your head?

Flossy

My Kingman saw me holding a hundred dollars! I was
tried to keep the money so I can get away from him.
I'm slowing down . . . too many of my friends have
been killed or are missing. God is trying to tell me
something, but I have seen countless miracles. What
do I need to be faithful?
(Flossy hands Sha some money)
Here, girl, I think you can use this.

(Brittny and Jelise are wearing headphones and stepping to the beat white horse.music They walks over to the other bench and sit) this is motion body language

Frank
(walking over to them and lifting one side of the bench)

(loudly) Roughnecks! Find your own bench. This is my bed tonight!

Sha
(approaches Frank)

Leave those girls alone and go get yourself a box. Girls, what are your names and what do we call you?

Brittny and Jelise
(they stand, put their hands in the air and gyrate with cruel body language)

Just call us the "High Rollers"! We will fight and step to you.
(Brittny shoves Sha)

Brittny

My sister, Jelise, and I aren't afraid of nobody! We been living on the streets seven years, ever since our mother left us.

Jelise

Yeah! The High Rollers are our family and friends. If anybody messes with us, they will be on you like bees to honey! And we aren't afraid!

(to Brenda)
Well, where are your High Roller gangs now,
roughneck? I guess they just fly high, rolled it up out
of here!
(Everybody laughs)
ZELWAURECO enters the stage. She approaches
Leland and hands him a brown paper bag containing
a butter peanut and jelly sandwich.

Zelwaureco
(to Leland)

I guess we're dining out again tonight. I had to wait
until someone brought out the trash.

Shamere

Mom, I'm hungry. What are we eating tonight? I wish
I had a McDonald's cheeseburger and fries.

Sha
(to Zelwaureco)

Excuse me, sister, could you share a piece of that
cheese biscuit with Shamere?

Zelwaureco

Sure! I have enough for everybody, a whole box, but
it's old. I had to knock a cat and a couple of roaches
off it!

Joseph

Hey, babe! Sound like more meat to me!

Frank

It won't be the first time we had roaches—gimme a
piece of that bread!
(Everybody moves to Zelwaureco to get some bread,
and Zelwaureco passes it out)

Jamario

Does anybody know where we're sleeping tonight? My
back is hurting on that bench! Will you give me your
socks? Mine has a hole and my feet are getting frozen
from sleeping outside.
I know—what about the malls?

Dorothy

We could always use the parks, or sleep in somebody's
car.

Sha

No, we can't! Because now they lock the gates, my
kids and I sleep at the "box hotel." I think all of you
should check in at this roach motel. The box motel is
free you know!

Brenda

What if we asked the church people to help us?

George

Those people look at us as if we have a disease! I
always heard

Baptists will feed a good meal on the first Sunday, and they can help pay your bills.

Alston

What bill? You don't have energy—light bill, remember? We didn't pay our rent because they kicked us out!

Joseph

Are you crazy? Look at us, we smell—hello! Those people will look at us like we have an infection!

Adrian

And don't forget, we're down and out. We can't go to church like this. They'll slam the door in our faces.

Joseph

What church or minister wants to help people like us? Do we look like Christians?

Adrian

After those church people take one look at us, I doubt they'll want us taking up the offering.

John

I know! We sure don't talk like "Christians."

Brittny
(to Jelise)

Girl, I wonder if God loves us enough to give us a
home. I wish we never left home. Where are our
so-called friends now?

Jelise

Girl, I'm tired of listening to you about those
roughnecks! Maybe we should have listened to our
parents instead!

Leland

Can somebody tell me why people treat us so bad?
I thought God loved all of us. May he's busy? Then
things might get worse or better? I don't care!

Brenda

God does love us because God lives inside us. God
had blessed me with a postal job, a salon, a car, and
a home—and I was big-headed. I stopped going to
church, turned my back on friends and family, and
lost it all.

Dorothy

I had it going on too, sister, with the money until
I decided, "Satan, you will not get me and be my
footstool!" Because God was moving too slow in my
life, yet still I am more than blessed.

Jamario

Then how come we have nowhere to sleep on
Christmas and we continue being homeless? Would
you say that is a blessing?

Brenda

We made that choice, not God. Sometimes God gives
us the rope to hang ourselves with. Things happen to
people to make them stronger.

George

Well, Alston, when you lost your family, did you get
stronger? When your husband left or after you lost
your money gambling, did you get stronger?

Alston

No, I got stronger after lifting those ragbags in the
trash. I could go back anytime because I got faith that
God will give me strength to overcome my problems.

Sha

Man, Alston—if you had faith, then why you would
not be scared to go home? Where is your so-called
faith now? Is it underneath that coat?

Alston

I need more than strength to walk back into that
house. I was dishonored to look at my children; I
need to refresh my life. I need a miracle. Do you think
God heard it?

John

Did we ever stop to pray and ask God for anything?
No! All we ever thought about was drinking, drugs,
gambling, money, and getting a good smoke.

Dorothy

You know, I never thought about asking God to help
me overcome my gambling habits; instead, I ask him
to help me win the lottery, but I learned that you have
to be careful what you pray for.

Adrian

Well, it is a bit chilly out here tonight, man! It will
take a miracle to help us. I sure could use a smoke and
then worry about someplace to sleep!

Lonnie

I guess we're sleeping on the icy streets again, in the
snow this Christmas, with the rats, dogs, and roaches.

Adrian

Hey, good-night, Frank and John.

Dorothy

(gets up off the bench and heads offstage)
Not me. I'm going to talk to that preacher from the
Baptist church because I'm getting too old to be living
on the streets.

Alston

(leaving with Dorothy)
Wait up, Dorothy! Reckon I need to talk to the
preacher about cleaning up what I messed up. You
reckon that preacher can spare some change for a
Happy Meal, bath, and clothes too?

Adrian

Go on, you hens, you smell like shit.
Go use a toilet far away and wash!

Frank

Yeah, and I need your bench! za

Shamere

Wait, Alston! Can I have your blanket?

Alston

Sure. I think the church will give me some warm
garments.
(Curtain closes)

END ACT I

❧   ❧   ❧

ACT II

(Curtain rises)

Sarah P. Murphy

That night, an angel appeared before Pastor Neal Jr. with a strong message from God. Pastor Neal wondered why he was chosen. God already knows all about us. Our lives are already mapped out. So when God gives you something to do, do it! If you don't want to see an angry God, don't question God. That night, God also sent an angel with a message to the homeless people. Meanwhile, "FIRST LADY" Maria Jones asked some of the members from Baptist church to go with the pastor. God has no favorite person to do his work. God can use anybody, anywhere, anytime, whether they are men, women, or children.

God said, "And a little child shall lead them."

(Sarah P. Murphy exits)
(Pastor Neal is asleep in a chair with his Bible in his lap. The white angel is Brittny)

Angel Brittny

(approaching and speaking to Pastor Neal)
Wake up; wake up—God has a job for you! Go and feed the homeless with knowledge and take your shepherds with you.

(Pastor Neal)

Angel, why me? What will I say to these people, and how will I lead them out of the streets? How many souls need redemption?

(Angel Brittny)

I am only God's messenger. Do not question God's
work. You are the chosen one. I believe God has
already given you the words to say. Believe that what
God wants is for you to trust him!
(Angel Brittny exits and goes offstage. Pastor Neal
drifts back to sleep.)

First Lady

(enters the room and shakes pastor Neal)
Honey! Honey! Wake up! You fell asleep. Who were
you talking to?

Pastor Neal

Honey, I had a visit from God's angel. The message
was to go out on the streets and bring his people
home. What will I say to these people, and how will
I lead them out of the streets? Inform Deacon James
and Reverend Florence. You need to tell them to bring
Sister Dorothy and Sister Alston with them.

First Lady

I believe you already got the words, and God has
already given you the assignment. Move as the Spirit
leads you to do, so rest tonight; there is work to be
done tomorrow.
(walks over to the phone, picks it up, and dials a
number)
Hello, Pastor Neal asked me to give you and Deacon
Vass a call. God gave him a vision to move forward
tomorrow. He has been commission to take God's
Word out on the streets and to take a powerful army

with him. He wants you to come with him, and bring
sisters Dorothy and Alston.

(Curtains close, end scene II. Stage is changed for
Scene III,
The Homeless)

(Curtain opens)

Sarah P. Murphy

That night, in the sky, a bright shadow in the form of
a white angel appears in the park before the homeless
with a message from God. Some of the homeless
people cannot believe their eyes. Some were still
sleeping in their boxes but they woke and began to
asked question. Had they understood an angel? They
wanted to know if the message was really an act of
God!

Angel Jelise

Awaken! Awaken, my children! God is sending one
of his chosen ones to help you. He will feed you
knowledge about God, my heavenly Father, and how
to accept him. Listen to this preacher, follow him, and
you shall never thirst or hunger again.
(Everybody talked amongst themselves, asking
question and saying things like, "Did your see their
faces?" "That angel glowed in the sky." "What was
that bright light?" "Where did the angel go?" "Was
that an angel?" "Was I dreaming?" "The angel had
wings!")

Pastor Neal

(arriving onstage; he pauses as he listens
to everyone discussing angels)
Hey, that's sister Dorothy and Sister Alston. Hello!

Joseph

Man, they look cute and bodies smell like perfume!
Who cleaned them up? They even have some new
clothes! Hey can you let a brother have a dollar?

Adrian

Can you have a cigarette roll-up! Man,
I know you have some money now, Sister Alston!

John

Hello Sister Dorothy. Who gave you that new wig?
Last time your stinking wig was most terrible!

Dorothy

Hi, everybody! You'd better get off that night train
and get on this Holy Ghost train. It is amazing what
God can do for a person just by asking.

Adrian

Hey, Sister Alston, who gave you those shoes? Does
the church have food?

Sha

Sister Alston, does the church give you an apartment?

Shamere

Sister Alston, have you sent any young adults to
ministry?

Dorothy

I am a member of the Baptist church, if that helps.
Look at what God did for me, and I didn't need my
husband to help me. God can supply it for you.

Alston

I am not sleeping or eating with the roaches anymore!
Nor do I have to sleep in parks, on benches, or in
boxes! God blessed me with a good, honest job. I earn
an income, and my lifestyle is reasonably healthier.
That is a blessing, thanks to the Lord!

Pastor Neal

I am Pastor Neal, and I have come to lead you out of
the darkness into the light. Take up your boxes, your
belongings, and do not look back. Move as the Spirit
leads. From this day forward, all of you shall have a
home.

Frank

You know, I don't know about the rest of you, but I'm
tired of living in the darkness. It's time for me to walk
in the light.

Flossy

I'm going back to church and tell God about my personal problems. God is only one I need to be acquainted with. I have spent more time on the streets than in the church.

Jelise

What light? It's already daylight. Man, I hope you mean a real home and not a hell home or a rejection. If so, I'm staying right here.

Jamario

Are you the minister the angel spoke about? You sure don't look like a preacher. Where's your Bible? Where's your robe or that collar the preachers wear?

Adrian

Yeah, man, what's up? I thought you preachers are supposed to be old! How do we know if you ain't one of them Jim J. preachers?

Joseph

Man, that ain't no Jim J. Do we look like we got money? I don't think so!

Deacon James

He's not like Jim J. A true man of God looks at a person's heart rather than judging him from the outside. We as Baptists cannot and will not judge.

Brittny

Are we being punished for our sins? Is that why
people run from us and mockingly laugh at us? Those
Christen people give us some food, clothes, and then
they talk about it.

Shamere

Yeah! Does God let his children starve day after day
until you die?

Pastor Neal

No, child, God loves us and frees us from our sins
by sending his son Jesus. Jesus shed his blood. He
died for all humankind so that we may live. God
wants all of us to live so that you may tell others of
his goodness! The Lord is alive in us, to trust and
baptism! God cannot use us if we are dead!

John

Is that the reason we can't find a warm place to sleep?
Or is it because God didn't hear us?

Frank

Does God love us even if we never went to church? Is
that the reason we cannot find a place to sleep?
God want us to come to him as we are, God has no
vision of what a "respectable" person should look like.
He want you, with your dirty|
clothes, foul-smelling body, alcoholism, prostitution,
and drug addiction.

Alston

He is unblemished! God wants the homeless to come in off the streets. Your testimony will be stronger in God's words.

Deacon James

We all may fall down. You may be tested in life with good and bad events, but the good news is, God has no favorite person, so trust him. He loves everybody! God can use you in a mighty way! God doesn't blab your business. He already knows your problems. Pray in your heart daily and call God about it. He is a good listener.

Leland

Does God love us if our faces are dirty and our clothes smell?

Deacon James

God can use each and every one of you in a mighty way! He's on his time!

Reverend Florence

Young man! God does not care what a person looks like, smells like, or what a person has; he loves us all. God is about love, sharing, and humbleness. God can take a drunk and make him leader. He can make somebody out of a no body. Just welcome God into your hearts and have faith in everything you do or say.

Deacon James

From this day forward, all of you are our family. We, from Baptist church, will welcome you and teach you how to live by the Word of God. Only one thing I ask of you, one thing, and that is for you to have faith!

Joseph

Hey, Pastor Neal, can God love me if I am a drunk? And can he heal me from drinking? Does God have that power?

Pastor Neal

Once you are in church, and you praise him, then you will understand his words. Example God can touch people and heal them, he can move or form a mountain, he can raise the dead. God's word can end this world. Yes, how powerful God is!

Reverend Florence

Keep your faith, stay in the Word, and you shall never hunger or be cold again. God has never turned his back on anyone. I cannot say everyday will be like Sunday, but the sun will shine.

Pastor Neal

You will be fed with the Holy Spirit, and then all of you can have all God's blessings. God is offering you a better lifestyle. Look at where you are now, and do not forget where you came from!

(The homeless people start talking and asking questions amongst themselves about whether to follow this pastor)

Frank

Hey, man, what do you think? Shall we go with this pastor?

Adrian

I don't know about wine and bread . . . unless he had light-purple drink?

Joseph

Like Kool-Aid? (chuckles)
Man, I'm thinking twice about it. I sure could use some hot food, a warm bed, and a pair of loungewear and pants! My wife tried to get me to go to the church, but all I wanted was money and women.

Frank

I don't know! I've been out on the streets for many years. I'm tied to the parks or places, so I need a change in my life. Who said it would be better to go any churches?

Leland

The angel said it; remember, she spoke of this pastor coming. Think about hot meals, new clothes, and schooling. I saw many other preachers and Baptists watching—but helping? Certainly not! They were afraid and looked away! I have so many questions.

That last preacher offered us redemption. I will look
at a real church family!

John

That helps enlighten me about who God is.

Shamere

Why did he die for us, Mom?

John

(looking at Sister Dorothy)
She has a real job, so I believe God can do the same
thing for me.

Shamere

(facing her mother):
Mom, I'm scared! What does 'the hour is near' mean?

Sha

God is giving us a second life. I know one thing—we
are tired of begging! Do you think Flossy and
Dorothy, those sisters at the church, could cook a
good hot pork chop dinner? God's way is better than
living out on the streets and fighting those bugs in
ours box motels. I and my children are willing to go
with this pastor!

Brenda

That's right, sister, Leland and I are tied of eating
leftovers after the roaches. My child needs spiritual

education and real nourishment. Think about this.
We tried it our way, and you see how we are living, so
why not try God's way?

Leland

(looking at Adrian)
Put that wine bottle down. Let's go with Pastor
George, Deacon James, and Reverend Florence. What
do we have to lost? Nothing! But Mom and I need a
lot to improve this life!

Adrian

(walks over to the trashcan and throw his wine bottle in)
I'm leaving this behind. As of this day, I am ready to
move forward. Do you think the pastor will help find
me a counselor? Who knows, maybe one will help me
find a job. I'm enthusiastic to try!

James Edwin Vass

(passing out apples in a basket)
Will all of you come to church with me?

Michael

(looking at his mother)
God does love us, so let's go into the house of the
Lord, and we will never be homeless again.

Flossy

(The phone rings and she answers. There is silence as
she is obviously listening)

Not tonight, I have a date with God. My nights are booked. I am tired of being out on the streets and offering my money to Kingman. As of this day, I am turning my life over to God. God is who I am taking my orders from now! Bye!

Cassandra

You know, making money the fast way is okay, but selling drugs is killing our people. When I became a registered nurse, I made a promise that I would save people's lives. I am going back to the church to help save lives.
(Everyone holds hands and forms a half-circle across the stage)

Pastor Neal

Let us have a powerful prayer. (He prays)
(Everybody applauds)
Thank you, Lord. What a joyful Christmas Miracle for the Homeless!
(Everybody sings Loud)
"Joy to the World"

James Edwin Vass

(passing out real apples from the basket)
I'm happy, Mom!
(Curtains close)

Sarah P. Murphy

This is end of our play.
(invites all the cast to come back onstage)

Remarks from the writer/creator

"For unto you is born this day in the city of David a Savior, which is Christ the Lord" (Luke 2:11, KJV).

Christmas is a joyful time, but many people do not know divinity. There are many people who are homeless but understand Christ died for us.

Christmas was an emotional time, where I didn't have anything, not even a home to live in, until meet a pastor who took interest in my needs. By him doing this, I then wanted to make a difference in other people's lives, to take the time and help the homeless. Maybe you too can help the homeless find their way home. All it takes is God, faith, hope, and charity, and with loving thoughtfulness and some time, you can help change the world. (That time is now!)

I give all the praise and honor to God, and we want to share with everyone that God is alive. I'd like to thank all of you for coming, and I'd also like to thank the actors, the performers, entertainment specialists (including my husband, Lonnie, and my son Lonnie K. I really couldn't have done it without all of you.

There are so many homeless people in need of shelter and food, but most of all they need people to care for and look at them as a person and to be treated as such. With every virtuous word, we need to read our Bible.

If you see an diseased whore, an incoherent patient, drunks, drug addicts, or homeless persons, don't talk about them, just help them by extending a hand and God will do the rest. Good night, and bless you all again!

—D. F. W. Alston, December 22, 2001

Children's Wish List Club

D. F. W. A., April 10, 2003
Designation
Dear Pastor:

I was motivated to write this letter to you. I was visiting the Hospitals Center on my way to the children's ward. I saw their parents who were waiting with their sick children. At that moment, I went to the floors where the children with disorders were staying, and they were miserable and were begging for Christmas toys. How sad their faces were.

I spent practically the whole day talking to the families, even ones whose children were smiling. Some children communicated that they wished they could go outside! One family asked, "Do you know anybody who needs services to receive help around Christmas and who need gifts?"

I explained to the family that this play was designed to cause awareness of the homeless, and this includes homeless children and sick children with no place to live. I was determined to make sure children will receive a happy, blessed Christmas. My mission was to distribute this money to needy families so the children can have clothes and toys. And for me, I wanted to offer thankful everyday gifts: health, education, smiles, love, belief, and to help the homeless.

"Jesus said to him, 'If you can believe, all things are possible to him who believes'" (Mark 9:23, NKJV).

The day before the play, I visited each home and asked each child what he or she wanted for Christmas, with the support of the Baptist church and this nonprofit. Your cooperation is very much needed and appreciated. I wanted to do something that would lift their spirits. I started thinking about how my family lived in poverty and worked manufacturing pickles, as housekeepers, and picking tobacco. (I remembered when I had one doll, whose name was Pearl. She was sad because she had a tear on her face! I had that doll for years. Then I collected unhappy dolls.)

I headed back to west end, and this was where a lot of underprivileged families live. I have a goal to believe in intelligence and education: to make sure we help our children.

"Dorothy Alston created sign on; October 17, 2001 Christmas Wish List Club with IRS employer identification numbers# 26-0015113.

"Application for *Children's Wish List Club*"

PO Box 1117
Henderson, NC 27536
Vance County Phone
Sponsoring Church Info:
Church's Name: "The Battle is God for the True Trinity Holiness Church of God"
Church's Address:
Contact Person:

Head of Household Name
SS#
Address
Phone #
County
City: State:
Monthly Income:

1. Child's Name (last) (first)
Date of Birth Sex
Shoe Size Shirt Size Dress Size Pant Size
Special toy request:

2. Child's Name (last) (first)
Date of Birth Sex
Shoe Size Shirt Size Dress Size Pant Size
Special toy request:

3. Child's Name (last) (first)
Date of Birth Sex
Shoe Size Shirt Size Dress Size Pant Size
Special toy request:

Parent(s) Signature: "Evangelist Omega A Williams", and sister (M.)
Date
Please return application as soon as possible.
   • Maximum 3 children from the same house to receive gifts
Names of Kids in Children's Wish List
   • Children's Wish List (Please place your name beside the number you pick.

Several families were helped from West End Community, Warrenton, Granville, Franklin, Louisburg, counties in NC. The Children's wish list was a huge success.

Introduction: Dorothy's Emotional, Spiritual Poems

Dorothy Faye Williams Alston is a Black woman who in 2004 recited a poem, "Dorothy's Dream," which was written at a rally for HM School honoring Dr. Martin Luther King Jr.

The play "Dorothy's Christmas Miracles for the Homeless" is self-confident, with high regard to the Children's Wish List Club.

"Let not your heart be troubled; you believe in God, believe also in me" (John 14:1, NKJV).

I hope to help people find shelter, food, and clothing. I have three children (Tasha, Brittny, and Lonnie) and three grandchildren (Tymere, Shamere, and Michael).We are joyful. We share conversations as a family, in places of worship, while bargain hunting, and while dining in restaurants.

After my back operation (which I describe in detail in my Introduction), a miracle happened! I eventually began to progress and wanted people to listen to my story. Because I don't want my writing to be futile, I wanted to be able to clearly express myself, so I began to pray and read God's work. This is where I want to acknowledge a special "guardian angel."

About two years ago, God brought into my life a great degree of organization that I afraid to ask to assist me. This guardian angel was kindhearted and spent time with me. She listened to what I said and wanted to help me achieve my goals. She said, "Dorothy, if you want to get your story out, then that is what you're going to do." I read my stories and poems and edited them to where I wanted them to be. "Guardian angel," I thank you again. I believe I will continue writing my stories into the future. I want to write about life's numerous stumbling blocks!

My motivation has always been God, and now I have even more material because of my life. There were struggles in the path of my conquest! When people read my poetry, they will know that I am a miracle, and that I am alive for a purpose, which is to testify to God's greatness to those who are lost so they can receive hope and faith and believe again. I want to let people know that no matter what may stand in your way, you have to press on. I'm in a better state now than ever before, and I believe I am victorious because God did it!

My question is where is the uprightness for people like myself? This is why I call this book *Dorothy's Poetry: Emotional Healing through Christ*. I have to trust God for my total healing. I hope even now as you read this you pledge to accept that there is only one creator, and God's Spirit and energy lives within us all. This poetry is about my journey within and the empowerment I received by denouncing man and exalting God.

I will be writing a novel about my complete life's journey, and it will be titled *God Told Dorothy: You Are Somebody*, which will be my autobiography.

WHAT IS THE TRUE MEANING OF CHRISTMAS?

For unto you is born this day in the city of David a
Savior, which is Christ the Lord.—Luke 2:11

I love Jesus every day, at during Christmas it's never-ending! Some people don't know the true meaning of Christmas, and I wonder why. Because when a period of abundance was higher, the world would be blessed with a holy child who was a female. "But when the fullness of the time was come, God sent forth his son, made of a woman, made under the law" (Galatians 4:4, KJV).

The True Meaning of Christmas
December 25, 2003

I believe woman was an angel
She trusted conception in her womb.
Her name was Mary
Her husband was Joseph
From Galilee it passed, centuries in those days
Mary about to bring life
She almost delivered
Governor of Syria wanted to taxed everyone
But Joseph didn't wanted to pay fees, so they left instantly.
They traveled many miles to a town called Bethlehem,
Mary's gift was about to be delivered.
They arrived at an inn, but there was no room.
The caretaker knew Mary was about to give birth
to her first son!
Mary and Joseph laid the new baby in a manger.
Bethlehem shepherds kept steadfast watch in fields
of their flocks throughout the night.
Suddenly, a guardian angel appeared, and the shepherds were afraid!

In Bethlehem of David, "Redeemer," which is "Christ the Lord,"
Will bring countless joy to all peoples!
Magnificence there was, with seraphim and a multitude of heavenly
majesty to God
now on earth!
Peace and virtue toward men!
Angels vanished, and shepherds offered praise as holiness came unto
the world!
The true meaning of Christmas is that Jesus was born!

Private Prayer: Healing Dorothy's Pain
December 26, 2005

*And the Lord will take away from thee all
sickness.*—Deuteronomy 7:15 (KJV)

Dear heavenly Father, I am . . .
It is I, Dorothy Faye Williams Alston calling your name.
I place all cares, relying on heavenly faith for a seed,
Who can heal all my pains.
Even at times, the woman "Dorothy" tried to be as good as you,
But now and then, it's an evil sickness of inferior quality,
aching to please clean me, give me healing.
When resting at the hospital bed, with aches and fevers,
Doctors, nurses, preachers were done, is what they said.
Every day I was depressed and the pills made me sick.
My stomach needed treatment.
Even though man cannot determine with 100 percent accuracy
a soundless God understood.
Even if I couldn't drop to my knees, Lord, it was me on at the
doorstep.
Help Dorothy with her silent, private prayer:
Heavenly Father, I have faith in your hand. Lord you're so close,

and you're here,
As sickness tried to drain my strength from my bones.
Please, Jesus, assist this diseased skeleton
While I am still in my household.
Faith is a private prayer as great as a grain of mustard seed.
I shall run, not drained of the body,
And I shall walk, still overwhelmed by the obstacle of pain.
Heavenly Father, grateful I am inside as you do the impossible.
Come in, so Jesus may possibly touch the hem of
my garment as I pass by.
I have the power of will to hold on, with praises and songs to God.
I am determined not let go until heavenly Father blesses
my body and soul.
Faith and a special private prayer will keep Dorothy safe
and help her heal.

Then touched he their eyes, saying, According to your
faith be it unto you.—Matthew 9:29 (KJV)

Saw Dark Pit in Mind
October 3, 2004

To you I will cry, O LORD my rock: do not be silent to
me, I become like those who go down to the pit.—Psalm
28:1 (NKJV)

Dorothy was a dark pit in my mind. I felt lifelessness with no
self-worth.
Dorothy isn't a machine. It was an error, like a broken switch control.
Now, she can read signs, but the blame was incorrect—
it was the "not knowing" of the mind.
Sometimes it makes me exclaim from the terrible pain inside.

I wish every morning when I worked and struggled that I had a 100
percent body.
Lord please help! The deeper, dark-pit mind struggles
because I declare good to be there.
I hurried helplessly against the evil spirit within me!
I released an unstable howl of horror, as if I was helpless,
and it sounded like a pathetic, undetermined destiny.
Has the world ended?
I *searched* for light but found nothing.
I reached deep within the mental strain for something, anything to
pull me through.
God, help me find self, feel a healing, controlled mind, and ensure a
complete moment.

*And he opened the bottomless pit; and there arose a smoke of a great
furnace; and the sun and the air were darkened by reason of the smoke of
the pit.*—Revelation 9:2 (KJV)

❧ ❧ ❧

Weakly Malicious Habits
August 12, 2007

Guardian angels, pastors, and fans
*Seek the Lord, and his strength: seek his face
evermore.*—Psalm 105:4 (KJV)

I fully believe and have faith, but I have had malicious habits.
I have frowned and shown violent annoyance. God, please support
your pastors and fans to overcome evil habits and have faith.

"So then faith comes by hearing, and hearing by the word of
God" (Romans 10:17, NKJV). So ask God to help Dorothy because
she needs requested ministers to preach for her, and pray to God
for help. I believed God sent a fearless minister to teach about the
righteous guardian angel who left Dorothy open to having faith.

"God is faithful, who will not suffer you to be tempted above that ye are able" (1 Corinthians 10:13, KJV). Your prayers helped me believe Dorothy now has confidence and deep truthfulness. I have promised God that I will praise him every instant, every minute, to walk in the light because God is worthy. When I put God first, he will provide my healings. When I was sick at the infirmary, it was your pastors and fans who prayed for me day and night. It helped me focus on these verses:

"And he said unto her, Daughter, thy faith hath made thee whole; go in peace, and be whole of thy plague" (Mark 5:34, KJV).

"And he said unto her, Daughter, be of good comfort: thy faith hath made thee whole; go peace" (Luke 8:48, KJV).

Ministers and fans you help improve inner faith to overcome mind and body. I shall believe the Lord! Daily I heal now. I'm grateful for the special pastor of the clergy, and your family has always been truly congenial!" You came straight from the Bible. I believe. I am told, "Don't worry, Dorothy, God will guide the path you are now on!"

Dorothy's Righteous Words of Comfort
June 3, 2001

Be not overcome of evil, but overcome evil with
good.—Romans 12:21 (KJV)

I am what I am. Expecting me to stop hatred, hurting, and nagging can injure my pride.

But God told me, "Don't hide your pride." God said to do good in sparkling his eyes, that it doesn't matter.

That's why I say when anxiety comes my way, just stand, don't shed tears because I am happy! I stopped the drugs and the hatred. It took a real man to help me.

Yes, when the enemy was wrong and loud and spit in my face, it doesn't matter—what is my color skin? I almost killed him!

God whispered silently in my ears and said don't be shy! Then I return with righteous words, relief for the enemy, and say expressions in a clear, full mirror.

Ask yourself, are you better than I? What's the reason for hatred in the world? Can you tell me?

❧　❧　❧

Lord, Our Family is Happy This Thanksgiving
November 26, 2012

Therefore I say unto you, What things soever ye desire,
when ye pray, believe that ye receive them, and ye shall
*have them.—*Mark 11:24

Happy Thanksgiving!
Praise you, *Lord,* even though some of our family is deceased.
On other hand, we're always alive, smiling happily, sharing memories!
We are joyful and indebted to you, God,
For happy thankful years, because you gave us to each other:
Williams, Alston, Haywood, and other kinfolk and friends.
I have hope that our family will continue to be blessed.
Lord, we give praise for our families
And are thankful for friendships that remain in God's path always.
Everyday God gives us a sunset that we love.
Our lives are with him and it raises life every single day.
Our family has so many blessings on Thanksgiving,
we praise God that he keeps ours family together.
People should stay closely connected to Jesus.
We are thankful, Jesus, that you bless our efforts to trust in love,
you assist us in your authority,
we hope to be worthy of your healthiness,
and always with a ration of strength

we wish to do mightily virtuous workings for you.
Enter into his gates with thanksgiving, and into his courts with praise: be
thankful unto him, and bless his name.—Psalm 100:4
Lord, we are thankful for you.
We remember special times and that our family is near and distant.
I love you.
Happy Thanksgiving.

❧   ❧   ❧

Now I am a Virtuous Black Woman
Dorothy F. W. Alston (Flossy 1) "Somebody"

May 3, 2003
I'm Dorothy, who was an adulteress
Guilty of a US dollar
I was prepared to take all risks
An elderly acquaintance offered me a ride.
He beat me, because "Flossy" betrayed him.
He tried to rape, but I stabbed him.
So, dagger—was Flossy wrong?
When I said no,
the knife slid inside his stomach.
So I cut off his fingers.
The man is a demon!
Was Flossy righteous?
Evidence stood against the accused during investigation.
Men spat on me; spoiled by royalty.
Some bad people's authority was erroneous and unfitting,
broken when shaken by man.
No wonder Flossy said, "Don't trust them."
Is a religious man's love real?
All around, Flossy said men sank in the ground like quicksand,
collapsed in the world, those who built steel walls.
They took the sinful way, but

now Dorothy is a virtuous Black woman.
Lively with God's solid words, and beginning with his
spiritual Holy Bible
she is reasonable, self-assured, virtuous woman.
Approved, blessed by God's right hand,
Fearful of men no more. God and I will stand side by side.
His words of comfort say, "It is I, God, in front and back."
I have been made stronger by the powerful protection of God's armor.
A twenty-four-hour shield is God's love.
Stronger in my mind, body, and soul, stroked by God's power.
How can Dorothy, a virtuous Black woman, go wrong?
Shielded by guardian angels, anointed head to foot,
now I rely on God's love with a solid, closed hold,
elevated to "Dorothy," God's faith moves forward and not backward.
Only to gaze each day upon a mirror to admire
who I am, willfully know,
to tell everybody that I, Dorothy,
am a virtuous Black woman.

Woman Surprise Pot of Gold Rainbow
April 17, 2002

*The rainbow shall be in the clouds, and I will look
on it to remember the everlasting covenant between
God and every living creature of all flesh that is on
earth.*—Genesis 9:16 (NKJV)

Once there was a woman whose name was Flossy.
She saw a prophecy in the clouds.
Forsaken, she was left floating up and down in small boat at sea.
Flossy went along, hungry, with nobody to talk to.
Her calendar said it was October 3, and she marked the days as
passed.

"Tomorrow will be, and I will wake at the crack of dawn and find my
pot of gold."
The next day Flossy woke, and what a vision to see:
a white angel in the clear, blue clouds
before a purple, white, yellow, blue, and green rainbow.
She began paddling and paddling, until she got tired and fell to the
floor boards.
When she woke, she detected the boat ashore, safe now
on new, olive-green land.
The spirits following the rainbow until she maybe will walk no
longer.
Flossy rested where she sat to think and began to walk again.
She knew she had reached the finish
because end the end of the rainbow would be a heavy pot of gold.
Finally, she said, "I reached the end of the rainbow and will run to see
my surprise!"
Flossy panicked. She saw a pot of gold inside a giant print!

❧   ❧   ❧

My Wars Are Communities
July 13, 2008

Because strait is the gate, and narrow is the way,
which leadeth unto life, and few there be that find
it.—Matthew 7:14 (KJV)

My wars are now in our churches, schools, courts, streets, homes,
communities.
I am parents of your friends and families, chilling in search of gun
thunder.
Not knowing who stands over my head with alien weapons,
factory jobs vanished across too many seas,
leaving us with pain relievers,
unwanted plants, foreigners being killed,

with me and my medications left with nothing.
Devil laughing in my community, avoiding our children with
undeveloped sexes, untrained, playing "guns"—why does anyone
care?
Mischievous sprites . . . so why are children killing their parents?
Afraid children don't respect their elders.
Tell us what happened, how men kidnap our children and woman.
Unsafe . . . taking longer to visit your neighbors
because we are scared walking in the light and at night?
Main-Street cops turn against combatants,
but who's in the wrong?
You must trust your right to be righteous.
My gang-bangers rendered to violate, pledged behavioral hatred.
I used to pledge my gang's currency,
exchanged for sexy, frantic liquors and rather insane pot-smoking
trips.
Now my community disbelieves people is their world.
My pledge is in my community and the world
because all children of God should believe!
My children are not slaves for the devil—families are free!
Fresh teenagers purify quickly, too passionately; newcomers to
abhorrence.
All because childish unseen are not malicious and should respect,
in my unity and yours, wars in your communities.
We must pray twenty-four hours with God to cleanse our
communities of war
and reached out then and there, clarifying, praising righteous land
before it's too late.
The world is infinitely God's.

"Yet I have set my king on my holy hill of Zion" (Psalm 2:6, NKJV).

Witness Payback
July 13, 2007

I witnessed particular adults and overwhelmed children open to being possessed by demons.

As a frightened child, my pain risked something coming inside me, a massive, unloved killer. If it tried, I knew something bad would happened. *Should I fight to the end? Who will win?* On the other hand, if as a teenager I left home, I could travel to an even eviler land! *Help me!*

I was unclean—witchcraft, murders, laughing party, and wrath, profanities, weakness, a sinned world—and Mom, you were right! It took me years and still ask God daily to forgive!

Dorothy offers improvement, seen in God's mind's eye! God work in me and does well! Witness was unpleasant, absent in hot rains under the netherworld. Imp had disappointments waiting for me.

My past grew in life into a wild mortal's world. I watched various children imprisoned by some and turn out to be sophisticated demons! I talked to a lot of youths through the years, but many elders looked away, so children became unsupported. My witness said I was the grownup for the parents who never bothered to practice, and education caused wrongs, left us unskilled.

I observed the elderly, children, youth in streets and some teenagers made eyewitness! We adults are spectators and need true eyewitness to share our children, watch out for them. Until then, appear on behalf of God for children whose good self-esteem should be given by their father and mother.

"Withhold not correction from the child: for if thou beatest him with the rod, he shall not die" (Proverbs 23:13, KJV).

"Thou shalt beat him with the rod, and shalt deliver his soul from hell" (Proverb 23:14, KJV).

"He hath said, I will never leave thee, nor forsake thee" (Hebrews 13:5, KJV).

❧   ❧   ❧

Dorothy's Twenty-Third Psalm Prayer

My section on Scripture was ready, when I felt
hardhearted, weak, and depressed.
It helps me to read daily Psalm 23:1–6.
April 10, 2003

Ears forward to virtuous words. I find comfort from goings-on.
"The Lord is my shepherd"
God is in the lights and Dorothy is a helper.
"I shall not want."
I must earn God's trust, because he cannot be bought.
"He maketh me to lie down in green pasture"
I learned to ask God pray before things happen.
"He leadeth me beside the still waters"
It was silent when Dorothy prayed and watched God, who spoke,
Pastor led Dorothy to the altar.
God's will is to serve only him, not other gods.
"He restoreth my soul"
God cleaned me from head to foot.
Indeed, God restored Dorothy to one piece.
"He leadeth me in the paths of righteousness for his name's sake."
I might have had made various mistakes
Remain not perfect,
but good news—
I promise to be God's servant.
"Yea, though I walk through the valley of the shadow of death"
God promised Dorothy would never be alone,
nor would he leave a frightened child.
"I will fear no evil"
"Fear thou not"
I know God delivers.
Put him first, and not myself.
"For thou art with me"
When I was blind in sin, God opened my eyes.
Now I can see!
"Thy rod and thy staff they comfort me."

Lord, I shall continue to learn and love in fellowship;
everywhere God is in the Bible
I make testimonies for studies.
"Thou preparest a table before me in presence of mine enemies:
Of mind weapon shield strengths surrender rivals"
God wants Dorothy to love and forgive one another
"Thou anointest my head with oil"
I magnify God's name eternally and praise with my cymbals and
dance,
I make a joyful noise.
"My cup runneth over"
I have learned to control my temper and close my mouth.
"Surely goodness and mercy shall follow me all the days of my life;
and I will dwell in the house of the Lord for ever."
Coming to the Lord is one thing I know was right;
he shed blood and died for you and me.
I live inside a light shining from the outside world.

❧   ❧   ❧

"Flossy 1"—God's Love Is Forever
January 11, 2003

Flossy 1's committed to God's love and with all humbleness, patience
in love.
A real lover knows without being told,
that God comes whole full of holes.
For reasons unknown the last man left thirteen years ago,
I trust no mortal man unless I can visualize a plan.
Flossy 1 was bound for husband until he found another woman.
Left her with two children—what was on his mind?
Flossy trusts no mortal man unless God shares a visualized plan.
Flossy cannot trust or love again, but I learned about God.
To heal helps, endless health issues survive,
the end of a loveless life is happiness.

Flossy said too much, for she had pain with nothing to gain.
Always husband never the same, distressing with his games.
That Flossy . . . he tried to drive insane.
Hard to believe husband was responsible, she was told
But you are liars.
"I don't understand, husband—why?"
"You turned away your head."
"I forgive you!"
God, look toward the sky!
Flossy gave you the sweet taste of a whole pie,
Trimmed down, waiting for you, honey bee.
Wonder, self-doubt . . . were those reasons you left?
Flossy, his woman got your money!
God doesn't classify a liar or a cheat.
God has compassion and forgives.
Husband increases his anger and widens his rules,
but God's love is not molded, credited, or sold.
God has guidance for the longsuffering.
Flossy 1 would rather have God's love, truthfully,
Because I know God's love is forever!

Lord Please Help Our Soldiers
April 3, 2002

*If it be possible, as much as lieth in you, live peaceably
with all men.*—Romans 12:18 (KJV)

My son is Lonnie K. Alston.
Please! Please help our soldiers' prayer for peace awaken in the world
and wait for the hope held upright by your faith!
I'm standing in the prayer line to talk to my son, Lonnie, and other
US soldiers.
Lord, I pray, anoint every soldier and their families' hearts,

Heal minds going back in time to March 19,
Before the countdown of war started.
Take soldiers and hold them, and do not let go,
Cover all branches by stretching forth your massive hand,
Guide their feet beyond sand and cool heat by night.
Would you, Lord, please, please, grab and shield each soul?
Let my son and our soldiers know, Lord, that this war will soon cease,
That you will keep us in perfect peace.
Heavenly Father, calm your storms, rather than more bloodshed.
Instead, tell Satan and our rivals to put down their guns,
unify with heavenly Father;
this battle is already won.
Because, Lord, you rejoiced in us too through war and serenity.
Yes! Lord, we toiled with differences of opinion and became spoiled.
The enemy is jealous of tools, franchises, and food.
Charge it to our head and not our heart.
Please, please don't hold our soldiers accountable! Escort them home.
Lift their burdens; merge nations successfully with the Lord;
Satan will become your birthplace until we collapse apart.
As I watch and talk about ours brave soldiers, my heart tears.
I pray continually for soldiers to read their bibles and believe
that if I had the ability or supernatural power, they would be back in
America.
Listen, heavenly Father, bless our soldiers in the desert.
Please help, Lord. I am crying, "What happened to our soldiers?"
Do they sound like self-effacing Egyptian children?
A peace rather than those rival men who are feeble-minded and
deceitful?
Now! God, which you have shaken US states and challenged treaties.
We are believers that God is first and last.
Lord, it is known we don't always do what we should,
But will you strengthen each heart weakened away from faith,
By letting our US soldiers on earth and in heaven know,
It's you, Lord, who holds authority, not man.
Lord, just one more thing:
Let rivals know that we are prayer warriors

Known as "The American Family" who
believes and has the faith of a mustard seed.
So take heed, rivals,
the United State will succeed, and our soldiers will be home indeed.
PS Sorry, Lord, this poem is long, but I wanted these soldiers to
know that from childhood to adult, I was considered a nobody. But a
miracle happened, and Jesus cares that I am alive.

❧   ❧   ❧

Mother Holds Various Jobs
May 13, 2001

A mother is a first-class woman of sciences, one who is burdened
with child. She creates offspring and can communicate educational
programs. She safeguards against the devil, cares and provides for
and helps her children when they are in a bind. After she has cleaned
her house, she cleaned the filthy laundry room. If she doesn't have a
vacuum, then she uses a broom. Your mother makes an effort to clean
in the morning because she knows the children will be home soon!
Your mother washes clothes for the entire family.

When family has a bad cold, your mother will wipe their runny
nose. Mother watches over affairs of her household. I remembered
when my mother cooked seven meals for her family in an iron pot.

Your children behave badly, but she looks at them with a smile
and says, "It's just a test." Everyday mother pray because Satan tries to
steal our joy, kills and frustrates and destroys bodies. For these reasons
your mother shields her child in and out of seasons.

Likewise, Satan tried to harm Mary, but Jesus rose three days later
and raised up.

Now, children you should purify every day, applaud and salute
your mother.

I want you to love your mother as well as share my happiness for
these six reasons:

M: Mothers always try to do what's best for us. If you have a mother you are truly, truly blessed. My mother died February 4, 2011.
"And he stretched forth his hand toward his disciples, and said, Behold my mother and my brethren!" (Matthew 12:49, KJV)

O: One mother hadn't smelled her flowers. Only one mother can't take her place! Give your Mother now, doesn't wait to smell her flowers. "The grass withereth, the flower fadeth: but the word of our God shall stand for ever" (Isaiah 40:8, KJV).

T: Teach me, Lord, to be a righteous mother to connect me with my children.
Teach them, Lord, how to grow in your terms. "Good and upright is the LORD, therefore will he teach will sinners in the way" (Psalm 25:8, KJV).

H: Honor your father and mother, children. This is the first rule in your home. Don't "mouth off" at your elders, and pay attention to your mother and father. "Honor thy father and mother" (Ephesians 6:2, KJV).

E: Every time Mamma turns around, the devil is trying to break up your family, and a demon is busy trying to achieve this at home, on your job, but your mother will pray and sing songs. "Thou therefore endure hardness, as a good soldier of Jesus Christ" (2 Timothy 2:3, KJV).

R: Remember, it was your mother who brought you into this world. Children should show her multiple kindhearted roses. Remember your elderly mother; take time and be extra careful toward her.

Someday your mother will die, like mine and many others who left to be in heaven, which is already a bright-blue world. They can never be replaced, but we must respect all elders if we are to live righteously; one day we shall see Jesus face to face.

I had this card for my mother, and I wept nevertheless; I am joyful; I am well-made in mind and body.

"Only they would that we should remember the poor; the same which I also was forward to do" (Galatians 2:10, KJV).

Brothers' Positive Changes
February 24, 2011

*And all things, whatsoever ye shall ask in prayer,
believing, ye shall receive.*—Matthew 21:22 (KJV)

I have two brothers, Designation and John, who are both God's miracle, marvelous men in this world. They have a positive outlook and are often happy, though sad memories happen too—they grieve for Mom, but we are joyful because she is in heavenly spirit.

Through more conversations we expose ourselves to family with a smile. We try to improve their lives here and in houses of worship, and we praise God.

Why it is important? Brothers are like their family. Kinfolk mean so much and primarily is a blessings. We applaud God everyday for his wonderful earth. Rejoice because you are alive. I believe my brothers are positive. Both of you change daily. Value time with God and pray always: love, hope, health, and vision.

Dorothy's Angel's Christmas Carol
March, 23, 2002

My name is Dorothy, and I live alone.
People used to gossip
and laugh about me
because I had no children,
or gifts under the tree.
I used to think maybe those people were right,
but now I know they are unsympathetic.
I believe God will send an angel boy,
a child come Christmas Day.
I will wait on God and will not grow tired.
Then I said to make sure those people are right with the Lord,

that not even Dorothy is believing.
Before asking for a child, God already knows her wants and desires,
even though fourteen years had passed.
I remained steadfast in prayer for a baby.
Yes, the spirit Holy will strength me as a guardian angel,
and will not get tired.
The time is now winter, with arctic snows just before Christmas Eve.
As I sat rocking in my chair looking out the window,
I clenched tightly to my Bible,
watching downhearted people walk by.
In silence I looked through a large, clear window.
I saw homeless people walking around,
with nowhere to lay their heads.
I sat up when I unexpectedly heard a jingle at the door.
I ran to open it. There stood a teenager boy.
He seemed about fourteen years old.
"Can I come in?"
He had father nor mother, and people had left him all alone.
Some people treated him as though he was a criminal.
I said I understood and said, "Indeed, come in,
please remove your hat."
His cheeks were red, and face glowed like an angel's.
He said how grateful he was to meet me.
"My name is Kang. What's yours?"
"My Christian name is Dorothy."
He looked depressed and had a foul smell about his clothes,
and a coat full of holes, and army boots with no soles.
I offered Kang an enormous bowl of chicken soup
and a steaming mug of hot chocolate.
God wants us to treat everybody with respect.
I asked him to sit and stay a bit,
but he said no, he was North Jersey bound.
I immediately went to the next room to call the call to police.
On the way back from the kitchen, he was nowhere to be found.
Was he real or imaginary?
Then a loud voice said, "Please be still."

My eyes widened.
A tall, attractive man with a humble voice smiled.
He said, "Hello, Miss Dorothy. Good morning.
This is Christmas, and I am from the adoption agency."
I thought it was Christmas Eve!
The man said they found a baby boy; an infant.
God works and I know I had to be still,
to be trustworthy and believe.
The man said the child's name is Kaschiel.
Now I knew it had been God knocking at the door!
It was God who send miraculous gifts, and it was an
angel's Christmas carol.

"I wait for the Lord, my soul doth wait, And in his
word do I hope" (Psalm 130:5, NKJV).

❧   ❧   ❧

Lord Jesus Was Crucified!

Jesus of Galilee is from Nazareth.
Who is this King? The Lord never judges by skin.
Yes! Jesus forgives all sins.
Lord formed man and turned him back to sand.
The Lord is recognized as one who uses hope to heal.
At that moment, Judas, who betrayed Jesus
(who was sold for thirty pieces of silver),
and the world know this is what he did,
our Lord Jesus Christ
to suffer to save children, women, and men.
Jesus died to pay our price for our sins.
Lord Jesus Christ died on the cross, led away—who knew his place?
He died not for Dorothy or you but for *all* people.
It was the third hour after he was crucified,
at the sixth hour, and darkness covered mountains and land,

everything stood still.
He howled, "Why?"
By the ninth hour, Jesus gave up the ghost.
Jesus is who holds tomorrow.
Jesus can wipe away our pains or sorrows.
I don't look back at yesterdays,
really watch to believe better days, and I pray.
This is everyday, all inhabitants should be glad-spirited
and learn to love in harmony.
All God's creatures want to be with Jesus.
I want all Christian to know what I know!

Crucified
March 3, 2002

C: "Come now, and let us reason together, saith the Lord;" (Isaiah 1:18, KJV). If I want to see Jesus, I must live the right way. I must do beneficial things for others and accept the consequences, if you want to reach God's kingdom.

R: "Remember the word that I said unto you, The servant is not greater than his lord." (Psalm 89:50, KJV). I must keep his word. Kjm m b
"They are all plain to him that understand, and right to them knowledge that find knowledge" (Proverbs 8:9, KJV).

U: "Unto you, O men, I call; and my voice is to the son of man. (Proverbs 8:4, KJV). Unless the need to change struggles with evil habits or the devil's will.

C: "Chairity suffereth long and is kind; charity envieth not charity vaunteth not itself;" (1 Corinthians 13:4, KJV). I will walk upright in a proper manner in God's house.

I: "If we say that we have fellowship with him, and walk in darkness, we lie, and do not the truth" (1 John 1:6, KJV). I let my vital light shine, and I need to see day with my own eyes.

F: "For he shall grow up before him as a tender plant, and as a root out of a dry ground (Isaiah 53:2, KJV).I must have faith, because my hope will hold on!

I: "I am Alpha and O-meg-a, the beginning and the ending, saith the Lord," (Revelation 1:8, KJV). Jesus went to the cross for us. I need to keep God's orders.

E: "Examine me, o lord, and prove me; try my reins and my heart" (Psalm 26:2, KJV). I will daily give the lord praise; make spiritual dances, sound trumpets, harps, and cymbals; therefore, I am motivated to make some noise. He is worthy!

D: "Deliver me, O Lord, from the evil man; (Psalm 140:1, KJV). When evil spirit are in my way, I say this is a stumbling block. What I do is get down on my knees and pray hard. Then I pick up my Bible and reread several verses.

Something to think about: What would have happened if Jesus had come down from the cross? It's wonderful to know he accepted the blame. None of us could have borne Jesus' pain. That's why everybody needs to magnify Jesus' name.

Jesus Cares for the Whole World
November 5, 2004

Children, Jesus wants you to obey your mom and dad.
We must put aside the anger and hate.
Jesus shed blood for everybody to show us the way.
Working together to help one another is the answer.
Let us tear down this brick wall, which is a divider.
Jesus was nailed to the cross, and not one word did he speak.
He cares for the world; he is charitable, loving, and
helps you recover your life.
He gives us peace, shelter, food, and more.
Not one man on this earth can do the things Jesus did.

It is wonderful to know Jesus cared,
Not one of us could have lasted with the discomfort.
Men, women, and children all need to know him.
We are not perfect like Jesus,
And yes, a parents' job can be rough
We should always be asking Jesus for strength
But let us not forget that Jesus is "the reason for the season."
I am glad to say, "I know in my life, Jesus still lives."
He makes many miracles when there seems to be no way.
Surely I can say, "Yes, Jesus cares about the whole world
and he is real."

❧   ❧   ❧

Dorothy's Expression of True Love
2000

Love is more for me than one vowed word,
Moves from emotions can be hopeful, whether
It shows expression, when heard
By Cupid's arrow shall not be missed.
Love at times can be expressed after acting stupid.
Breaks sometimes can't be fixed.
Love should never be disliked or bargained for sin,
For me, love almost caused a suicide attempt.
But today I have faith; you don't need money to buy love,
and I can't have any faith without hard work and love.
Love and faith are honest hard work.
Life will always have destructive negative pains,
As I have known many days' worth of sobbing and sad times.
Once hated to love, as love was like a thunderstorm,
It left me shattered in tiny pieces like a bomb.
But I listened and hummed loudly to gospel tunes—
God don't want me to sit waiting or weep proceeding
but to believe powerful prayers and then seek

the Lord's help for me to believe
by understanding how it's all connected.
Thanks, dear Lord. In order for me to have true happiness,
I must believe.
Yes, having the right heart makes me a soldier,
Working at my best, so nothing will go wrong.
Wait, wait—remember me always—I must pray, and clench, don't
ever give up,
hold on forever to God's right hand.

Dorothy's Hopeful Vision
January 3, 2000

I hope this dream of all mankind, quenching,
Reaching, taking place behalf at times.
Man wanting to be noticed. Soon to confess to being
"the Holy Bible."
Always running, scared of being "left behind."
Someday, God's children will unite.
All preachers addressing God's word will stand—
Nations, pose together, men to men.
Working, tilling our native land, does not worry dry all tears?
God will be waterless.
Man do not have the upper hand, know that God is man, do not fear.
We must be supportive and hopeful of this dream.
Yes, dreams come and go, and God's visions brings all mankind hope.
On God's word men shall stand, hand in hand,
dispensing guns and drugs,
Moving forward not behind for selfishness of money.
I dream all mankind kneeling as God's servant.
To motivate minds, stimulate hearts, and wake up souls,
Making sure we receive God's nourishment.
Concentrate continuously on God to heal us, mend all embraces.

Clutch a child not in denial, treat it with care.
Men's body and soul bonded to a woman's sides.
Man cultured about its preys, learns God verifies who dies or stays.
I stand positive in visions further of tranquility, harmony, and liberty
to show no hate.
Learn to love for our children's sake.
All roads are greediness to man is hell pit when it comes to a race.
Truly working mankind together widens narrow roads and paves,
forgives, and forgets.
Look at the world by season's signs, giving to all courage.
Take God's rules and move forward with patience, not fastness.
Man is fellowshipping better,
a journeying, peaceful agreement,
both knees praying toward sunny heaven,
nations' conversation must continually rise up to God's side,
breaking bread and wine with one another,
recognizing God does not hide.
Men need to talk to a companion, but not a chatterbox.
Family's disagreements put out a nagging child
with only negatives left.
It is time to stand up in fellowship and pray, fathers and mothers,
give your sons and daughters to hugs and neighbors.
Yes, all houses of worship and holy sisters
seek affection from all God's creatures.
We as human beings still haven't met Dorothy's hopeful vision.
Let's start currently and work in unity.
I'm only one person but will continue on the road to dream
until vision is clear and the time is near.
Remember to keep in mind God truly will not tolerate
pain and violence.
I have an upright dream that time is running out.
God is ready to stretch forth his right hand for people to believe.
"For yet a little while, and he that shall come will come, and will not
tarry" (Hebrews 10:37, KJV).
"But we are not of them who draw back unto perdition; but of them
that believe to the saving of the soul" (Hebrews 10:39, KJV).

Then, men will no longer have control of this world,
so let's begin today.

Healing Unity Marriage Is Commitment
January, 23, 2000

The day was hot on Sunday, August 31, 1986.
I was late for the wedding but it was a good evening.
Later, in 2000, the marriage broke.
I was left speechless, wanting to sing "We Will Be Together"
but instead . . .
here is a healing poem.
We said for each man God made man and woman,
Both husband and wife are committed in unity.
We wanted our marriage to last forever,
but healing a marriage is sharing responsibility:
yes, unity needed support—good and bad—
healthiness and sickness, grieve deeply, contribute financially,
may this seed prayer grow virtuously by accountability.
Marriage is obligation.
It takes two, for, "Let the husband render unto the wife due
benevolence; and likewise also the wife unto the husband" (1
Corinthians 7:3).
God truly wants us in the direction of work healing unity.
Endlessly believe God's trust is heading in the right direction
and shall strengthen us in friendship, not disbelief.
Hopefulness brought us to repeated conversations with God,
so tomorrow's unity is kept continuous toward a deep growth.
Marriage is happiness and gratification.
God insight—healing—is good for unity,
gratefulness is a trademark in marriage toward commitment.

Flossy Hot in Hell!
September 10, 2000

Life was trapped in large sphere of influence.
It's understandable—not all exoduses are clear.
A hot object—a pistol—I'm shot in the face.
Flossy tried to escape, in at W. E. hung around, can't keep hurting.
Locked in the hospital for six months with nothing to say;
crushed into a hold below in the underworld to hell.
The man pulled the trigger yesterday, my face melted into my mouth,
Spinning around in my mind like a merry-go-round,
Neither believing—what's in sight is imaginary.
Realizing I'm fenced in.
Hot hell, not knowing where I'm bound.
"But thou, O Lord, art a shield for me; my glory, and the lifter up of
mine head" (Psalm 3:3, KJV).
"Lord I need a breath of clear air to graceful days,"
Tiny, like a mustard seed, testimony.
Surely God, thank you. See? I do believe.
Now every day I open my mouth and say,
"Praise God come into the morning."
Without any crying encouragement, Dorothy heals and dries all tears!
For the moment, I'll wake up remembering always to pray. Take heed!

God Created a Woman
October 3, 2003

*Trust in the Lord with all thine heart; and lean not unto
thine own understanding.*—Proverbs 3:5 (KJV)

God prepared man for woman.
He shaped and molded me with clay and sand
and then blew life into my nostril

and gave me understanding and knowledge.
God is the crown as well as the body;
I read my Bible and obey God's word.
Dorothy is superior over the household;
nevertheless, I must be right before God and children.
Divinity wants me to have a true, pure heart,
I need self to be on both knees and nod.
But man's world has not learned who is the prey?
Spirituality wants me to love and forgiven, not hate.
God does not want Dorothy fighting your brothers or sisters,
enemies turn cheeks; fellowships pray when there is trouble.
I spread marvelous gospel according to God's Word,
Testimonies saw me, who has received redemption.
The devil had offered me wealth, power, and greatness,
but if I want to see God's face, Dorothy must have humble grace.
God praises the creation of a new woman and
does it with true fullness.

Dorothy's Happy Fourteenth Anniversary
August, 31, 2000

Lonnie knew we would have our ups and downs.
But it seemed just like yesterday that we hurried to the church,
hearing the wedding bells.
Patience, thirteen groomsmen and flower girls to see
my handsome knight
He stood at the altar, waiting for me!
Too much liquor before the wedding . . .
I felt sick, like Dorothy was duped,
the woman who was a queen.
We may always be together because we were meant for each other.
Let's forgive the past,
though we needed prayers and spiritual advice to start over.

Fourteen years is a lot of years to toss away communication.
After all sickness, God put us together to stay.
I will always forgive you, love you, but then virtue is the right way.
I chose God and his Word, which is true.
With love, always.

"Imaginary Lover
August, 7, 2001,

My lover knew without asking.
I thought he was unscratched, without any holes.
The last man wondered thirteen years ago.
To the streets I am bound; he found another woman.
Leaving two children—where is his mind?
I trust no mortal man unless I visualize a plan.
Working with reality, man is an ordinary dream.
I dream of an imaginary lover, warmhearted and smart,
vital in all goals; now I am separated,
lonely, single, and then I always will belong to your heart!
Working toward a kiss, not fighting,
I promise our love affair will work,
but only by communicating and not hating.
I base love on faith, trust, and honest.
Of course there will be mistakes, but remember:
it makes a secure relationship.
None of that he said/she said, or so I'd been told.
I do believe my imaginary lover—God—
will win him over with passion!
No shacking, no smacking—I learned a strong relationship
is built on trusting God to help build a strong family.

Help Broken into Locked Room
September 11, 2002

Rejoice evermore.—1 Thessalonians 5:16 (KJV)
No longer confined in a lonely hospital room,
As thy trotted back home, I almost died.
Don't wanted to stink. I smelled apple pie.
If scent meant something—rotted, heavy cast of my dead bones.
Thy stop to rest thy aching, burning feet
Self was broken down to my house for herb tea.
"Come in, nurses—is thy nowhere to be found?"
Down to Mrs. Brenda's room thy hear "door sounds."
Thy knock but the door was locked, but can't get out of the bed.
"Mrs. Dorothy! Mrs. Dorothy! You home?"
Moved 'round about to have a look-see at window.
Record player plays over and over my song.
Rocking chair rocks, stops in my room and an echo goes
"tick tock, tick tock."
There's nobody in the room after dark, and nothing moves,
Suddenly! "Help! Lord Help me!"
I felt a cold door . . . whole body (mine) still against the floor.
"Oh no! Hello!" It's God, on time!
Mrs. Dorothy answers, "God, I pray, strengthen me!"
Brenda says, "Who gave permission for you to leave out of your bed!"
Me, after willing God to call my neighbor.
What better time to call the police!

❧   ❧   ❧

Memory of Red A
June 21, 2001

Memories of Red's affection and care; yes, friend, thinking of you. This world was a test but you're at peace. God makes no mistakes. For no matter how much time passed, you will always be my first real lover.

Remembered spirit disappears, someday God calls us. It's too good to wait, but believe we are glad God called him to heaven. I don't miss the beatings, lies, liquor, and drugs! You battered me black and blue and left me on the street. I worked from nine to five to forgive and forget.

With you it is more than special memories, Red A. We had happy times, saw good and bad, saw the release of pain. No doubt. I will not forget Red A.

"Judge not, and ye shall not be judged: condemn not, and ye shall not be condemned: forgiven, and ye shall be forgiven" (Luke 6:37, KJV).

Obviously I am annoyed with the battle, but it is positive to forgive! Your true-to-life, beautiful testimony always rings true, sharing at this instant your tribulation to God.

Good-bye, Red A. Until we meet again in paradise.

Have Faith in Your Pastor
December 10, 2000

Be ye therefore followers of God, as dear children.—Ephesians 5:1 (KJV)

Blessed is a man who I found, a pastor who gave me good doctrine.
Personally I must go to the church
and don't sit at home.
How shall I hear without a preacher?

From your children to the elderly, your pastor is your teacher.
We must listen to every word when your pastor gives a sermon.
I have learned from his righteous words it is God we must seek.
This man was preached straight from the Holy Bible.
So don't wait until church has its revival
when preaching after a sermon focuses on prayers.
If we trust in the Lord, we can't go wrong.
His preaching has saved many souls.
I know this for fact, not just what I have been told.
I shall share my testimonies with others about what God has done for
me.
Pastor's responsibilities find souls in hospitals, nursing home,
on the streets, in jails, in subways, and in homes.
We as shepherd and church members must help make God's kingdom
now.
Pastors teach us to love one another and forgive.
Your community and world should help our sisters and brothers.
God will send one shepherd despite overwhelming numbers of
religious paths.
"I will save all souls and will not sleep."
There is one God.
Must have faith in your pastors, know God shall.
Whenever you have time, please come.
Then you will see.
Who can this pastor be?

Tasha, Brittney, and Lonnie Together are Virtuous

For we walk by faith, not by sight.—
2 Corinthians 6:7 (KJV)

I pray every day for inflection, gratification, satisfaction, that they have an achievement the size of a tiny mustard seed! My children are concealed in their lives. They are close, should be inspired but force the truthful words. You maybe know the self-possessed, up and down, tougher. Believe in yourself. I trust in life you discover God loves you, and have faith in yourself. Ask the Lord for grace first and then have it always.

Communicate, organize happiness and joy, and share huge smiling faces. You hold the ability to always handle technical changes in your life.

My children are creative, positive, charming, lovable, and very attractive. I pray for them together first and last important: "Whereas you do not know what will happen tomorrow. For what is your life? It is even a vapor that appears for a little time and then vanishes away" (James 4:14, KJV).

Believe the Lord's grace works daily, so rely together on life, and move toward the heart to achieve your goals!

They easygoing are virtuous and will vision the future from end to end a high, smooth, straightforward path. Always put Jesus at the head. Your strength is from the Lord, and with his mighty hands is the real power: when Lonnie, Brittny and Tasha have emotional problems, they connect with the Lord!

Deep Dark Hole
April 6, 2006

Who cares about me, indeed—
poles and bolts are heavy in my back.
I was chosen to carry this burden.
No one to help, I must be unyielding and bold.
Left alone in a dreary, tiny, deep, dark hole.
Time has come, and I am getting away from the past.
I endured years of suffering,
hoping all would live and there would be no pain.
Oh! How I wish I could see my late mother's joy,

gathering family, seeing reunions, loving them,
with no one left to raise your spirits.
No one to fault, but identity is to blame.
It won't be long until we meet in heaven.
I wish I could stay to tuck Mom in her bed.
But we must wear spirited smiles to face the world.
"Blessed are they that mourn: for they shall be comforted" (Matthew
5:4, KJV).
If Satan comes near me, God will attack him.
"Then said Jesus unto him, Get thee hence, Satan; for it is written,
thou shalt worship the lord thy god, and him only shalt thou serve"
(Matthew 4:10, KJV).
What worries us is that evil spirit will consume the elderly and
children.
Moving fast with a suit of armor,
we surely need our Bible and then a good verse.
Stay away from untrusting, negative, mischievous acts and walk away.
I used to see only a dark, deep hole,
but now I have diversity. I see a sparkle of positive!
At the instant I am alive
and knew spirit to be the same, I knew.
Brightness wears seasons,
and virtuous families will hear from God
about how I struggled and overcame.

Made Stronger Faith
April 6, 2007

Faithful is he that calleth you, who also will do it.—
1 Thessalonians 5:24 (KJV)

Praise heavenly Father, please give assistance to Dorothy. When I am humble, I pray for the chance before I am passed over get to my feet at the cross. I place all belief and confidence in improving that which makes my faith stronger. I am the woman who is in a weak, infirm body of disbelief.

"And he said to her, 'Daughter, be of good cheer; your faith has made you well. Go in peace'" (Luke 5:48, NKJV). Magnificent Lord, bless and heal all my cares and worries. I cannot totally recall sickness and pain as it tries to drain the strength from my bones. Please help ease the weakness, Lord, as I am nearby and grabbing hold of your garment.

"When she had heard of Jesus, came in the press behind, and touched his garment" (Mark 5:27, KJV). I will not let go until while waiting for God to bless skeletons. Surely I have a personality with an endless wisdom, where I "succeed." God is worthy of praise and made me find a solid faith and insight! Thank you, Lord, it's good to know you!

~☙   ~☙   ~☙

Why Must America Fight?
April 8, 2003

Prove all things; hold fast that which is good.—1
Thessalonians 5:21 (KJV)

America was once a country that showed no hate,
until an evil man from Iran became jealous of the US nation.
His nation made tools of wood, bricks, and sticks to edify at a faster
pace.
People build steeples and bridges, which others tried to take,
but within seconds, civilization became helpless.
Refused to drill or come up with ideas.
Rather, our nation was on hold, to aid other souls.
From invaders did faults they got over-the-top building killing
blameless people.
Intruders surge, merge and then America's dream became real.
Invaders started fighting wealth,
but America mumbles lyrics rather than words and said yes,
song of peace!
"What happened to America—we became weak?"
People were tapped, slapped, hit by thunder—
all because we are humble!
The question remains: "Why must America fight?"
Hush! Listen to thundering, thousands of people were weaker,
Collapsing, smell of humanity's flesh, lying at each other's feet.
Wealthy cannot be seen when bodies lie dead—
Lord, we need somebody to help!
Singing's power explodes at Mother's howl from the 911 attack,
President, yes—doing what is best!
People murdered, some hurt, not knowing what hit their back!
Others buried deep beneath pavement and flint,
People were lost, families don't knew their names.
Spirits wakened by families shaken with pain!
Families and homeless left with cocaine to easy their pain,
Americans become enemies rather to die to hell,

and this is why our US soldiers were sent to Iran.
We as Americans can serve our country, reducing hate,
loving our men, sons, sisters, brothers, fathers, and mothers.
Civilization does not need to hurt or turn guns on each other.
Are Americans better than the terrorists we slaughter?
If Americans want tranquility, US soldiers take out our enemies.
Dispenses all weapons, soldiers win; you are doing what is right: fight.
Harmony for our children and Iran's children's sake.
Please, God, help us. We pray for peace, hopefulness, and faith,
and we are grateful at this instant across the world.

Betrayal—a Late Evil Night
August 30, 2002

*And it shall come to pass, that whosoever shall call on the
name of the Lord shall be saved.*—Acts 2:21 (KJV)

This was August 31, 19xx . . . hot summer, late at night
Needed rest beneath a willow tree,
walking, sweating, dreamy as can be.
Suddenly, I am at the beach,
falling, partying loud, laughing under alcohol on arrival in Jamaica.
Admiring waves, riding cool, salty seawater,
Smelling cooking trout, deep-fried coconut oil.
I am listening, dancing, adult boobies dancing.
Loran shouting "wild white horse, no children!"
Run slow, unbutton, rotate, stamping disloyalty
and then tasting a small drink of old Jamaica rum.
Quietness brought forth darkness creeping low, elsewhere, on each
back street
a white guardian angel appeared, a vision
of dishonesty—to please stop the drunken insight.
Heard a loud roar and then winds raising high.

Dorothy yelled "wait!" An imagined voice was calling for quiet!
Remember—Do you know who creates the moon, birds, air, soil—
does anybody know?
Noiselessness transported into the world doesn't forgive me.
Darkness creeping beyond a high hill.
He was taken from prison,
and a gentle voice said, "Peace is still."
God's blood at the cross dripping, sprinkling from head to foot,
comes together forming a four-figure star.
God's eyes twinkle through stars at night,
yes, I must remember the anniversary,
and Jesus is the star—a bright light.

Almost Hellfire
August 15, 2003

Sleeping in bed like a baby child,
Awaken, face flushed red
What smoking has happened in hell—or am I in a dream?
Somebody shake me before I wet the bed,
and then a mighty breeze blew in like a powerful wind.
Fast fire paces up the walls,
Mountaineering reaching almost to the top,
Heat melting everything—no, please stop!
Like be locked in to cannot move darkness pit,
I prayed to the Lord:
"As for that night, may darkness seize it" (Job 3:6, NKJV).
sits touching this night on my face, the heat closer, quicker,
traveling more rapidly, speeding in the direction of room.
I heard feet working until collapsing, almost hell, this fire,
almost swallowing fullness like *Moby Dick*,
gasping ashes and smoke, running out of every breath.
Suddenly, a hero, a strong, mighty right-hand God pulls me up,

Stretching out God's touch entirely of branches,
Love embracing, squeezing, removing all thorns.
After morning healing comes a high of self-worth.

Main Road Miracle
November 9, 2005

*And having this confidence, I know that I shall abide
and continue with you all for your persistence and joy of
faith.*—Philippians 1:25 (KJV)

God's grace took place at the right time.

On November 29, Dorothy "Flossy" Williams Alston was driving one rainy morning while out for a double cheeseburger at a local restaurant. Flossie's car was swerving from side to side while she was trying to avoid a large puddle. Her tires slipped on the ground. Flossy was terrified and shocked—*What if the car catches fire?* She wondered. When the car flipped several times and crashed into a tree in an embankment on the side of road, everything stopped, and she was pinned inside. Silence.

Thank God a car driven by "R" was in the right place at the right time. He had to swerve to keep from getting hit. He saw her car flip into the embankment.

Suddenly Flossy was calling for help. God sent her two male guardian angels and a lady, came to her aid, and she sings their praises.

Flossy begged and prayed for anybody to help her, and her life flashed before her eyes. *Is this the conclusion of my life?* she wondered.

Flossy firmly believed God was watching her. The miracle was for her to remain still, to know God would be there in his time!

Flossy said Christmas was made blessed and extraordinary, and it would be quite a happy New Year!

God sends angels twenty-four hours a day to assist us. She wants us all to be thankful.

Flossy called her rescuers Mr. R, the designation man, and her Christmas angels.

❧　　❧　　❧

The Prizes Come at the End
October 3, 2002

Let love be without dissimulation. Abhor that which is evil; cleave which is good.—Romans 12:9 (KJV)

I can spread out the "prizes" at the end to loved ones. We aren't counting measurable prizes from men but in eternal prizes, through our life with God. May we grow seeds into blessings of happiness! Teach us the prizes in the world and strengthen our families!

When our loved ones die, nothing my family says or does can heal its pains. But I know a friend who can heal our hearts and wipe the tears from our eyes: tell it to the Lord! Mom and our lost loved ones will be sorely missed.

God always helps the needy. My sentimentality will testify how Mom touched others in her life. Physically she has moved on—God blissfully called her home. The battle had been accomplished, and her prize was to reach the summit with the Holy Spirit! We confidently set our hope for a prize in God! Though our stealthy request knows all, Lord, Dorothy's hopefulness will be allowed! We believe God's work is a reward of grace, and we are free from our sins.

"Wherefore is there a price in the hand of a fool to get wisdom, seeing he hath no heart to it?" (Proverbs 17:16, KJV)

"He put all things under his feet, and gave him to be the head over all things to the church" (Ephesians 1:22, KJV).

Dear Family and Friends

Thou believe that there is one God; thou does well: the devils also believe, and tremble.—James 2:19 (NKJV)

I would love to thank you for sharing your trustworthiness with me. I wanted you to understand several reasons I felt discomfort and hopeless. Why does it care? Why put the negative, brokenhearted events of my life into writing my book? This has been a hard road and a negative path. It's been hard to find relief, but, yes, God cares!

Now, Lord, with your love and absolute serenity, you have made me positive and have healed me going forward.

I am grateful for you in my life. May the Lord bless and keep safe each and every one of you:

1. Lonnie M. Alston; Lonnie K. Alston; Tasha Williams; Brittny Alston; Roberta Powell; Nannie Hargrove; Brenda B. Neal; Ethel F. Vaughan; Mildred Vass; Rosalind W. Wiggins; John M. Turner; George K. Vass; Natalie Watkins; Mary A. Jones; Lizzie Hart; Jacqueline G. Baskett; Lennie Harris; Patrice A. B.; Delthine Watson; Robert and Bernice Reavis; Johnny Watkins; Rhonda R. Hollowell; Marie Jones; Don W. Poole; Geraldine Moses; Patricia Bonita Kearney; Alfreda Mcknight; Carolyn Bullock; Louise Davis; Ricky Robinson; Mary G. Rick; Cecilia Alston; Faye Jordan; Zelwaureco A. Hill; Patricia Bonita. Kearney; Leroy Moses. Jr.; John Haywood Jr.; Sabrina Bate; James Harris; Hope Hall-Wilson; Glady Bethea; Cassanher McBurrough; Robert Bullock; JT Richandrson; Angela Mitchel; Nicholas La Raia; Kiziah Harris; Latonya Hayes; J'mia Knox; Brenda K Young; Elizabeth Hicks; Crystal Harris; Nannie Hargrove; Michel Bullock; Lillie Henderson; D. Hawkins; George M. Daye; Zarrie McBurrough; George H. William; Lola Turner; Mark Turner; D. Branch; A. Clements; Patricia R. Smith; June Seward; Munther Tabet; Barbara L. Parham; William H. Wiggins; Edith Hare; Annie K. Cousin; Hattie J. Cook; Helen T. Jenkins; Ethel A. Walker;

Rosa lee Mann; Kitty Freeman; Mary Louise Stewart; Ada T. Clifton; Clara Haywood; Hennetta Haywood; Shirley Kinton; James Edwards; Kita J. Terry; Angela Williams; John H. Neal Jr.; Leland Neal; Patricia (Trick) C. Ellis; Carolyn N. Hargrove; Patrick Hargrove; Jessie Hargrove; Simika White; Josephine Alston; Regina Hawkins; Justin Shane Blalock; Lettie Chews Talley; Lashay Beulah; Katie Clifton; Lykesha Ragland; Paul J. W. Tawney; Charissa McBurrough; Toney Marrow; James Harris; Angelette Hart; John W. Wryht; Lakisha Richardson; Mary Perry; Lakia Jones; John Haywood; Ruby Ann Harris; Rusty Bruskill; James E. Vass; Reverend Florence Cheek Vass; Jamario Deuon Vass; Louise H. Williams; Billy E. Williams Sr.; L. L. Bartlett; Victoria P. Bartlett; Ronnie T. Williams; Betty Jefferson; Willie Session; J. Henry Bank; Terry E. Garrison; Elton B. Vass; Mary H. Richardson; Fred Williams; Faye Anderson; Mrs. Barbara Jean Jiggetts; Shirley Jean Winbush Adams; Louise Jones; Jeanie Galloway Jones; Linda McFadden; Constance Davis; Gladys S. Brown; Joan Barnes ; Lois Finch; Tony Finch; Dezzie Durham; Maimouna Suye; Gnagna Samoura; Malissa Elkerson; Nancy woodruff; Joseph Ashley; William Felts; Garland Davis Jr. ;.Sarah Johnson Rosa B._Stainback; Early Moss; Shirley B. Tally; Joseph P. Lewis; Oumoum Bouye; P. Sonia Towa; Lelestine Wilkeson;. Evelyn B. Brame; Chet L. Swing;.

I hope you enjoyed reading my book, because my life contained certain responsibilities that I probably should have walk away from. I saw men in my heart who were extremely irresponsible and hurtful!

I saw a clear glass window about my life and beliefs, and the birds flew in season and chirped their songs! My new songs now!

"Whereas you do not know what will happen tomorrow. For what is your life? It is even a vapor that appears for a little time and then vanishes away" (James 4:14, NKJV).

When my life was heavy, I was determined at the crossroads. My beast inside said possess tight!, and I used to feel like giving up because my life at that point had already ended. This old body went downhill to men's lying words, but God received me new in faith and mind. God's seal is true. I found God, had him at no charge, so I talked, healed, and had the will to go on because God said to. Now God is alive inside me, and his will makes this a smooth journey.

"Then Jesus answered and said unto her, 'O woman, great is your faith! Let it be to you as you desire.' And her daughter was healed from that very hour" (Matthew 15:28, NKJV).

"And Jesus went about all Galilee, teaching in their synagogues, and preaching the gospel of the kingdom, and healing all manner of sickness and all manner of disease among the people" (Matthew 4:23, NKJV).

"In the midst of the street of it, and on either side of the river, was there the tree of life, which bare twelve manner of fruits, and yielded her fruit every month: and the leaves of the tree were for the healing of the nations" (Revelation 22:2, NKJV).

Don't give up on the Lord. Converted servants of God and achievers of everlasting life: How can you heal yourself when only the Lord can touch you?

ABOUT THE BOOK

My purpose for writing *Dorothy's Poetry* was to share the feelings that words alone could not express. My inner pain was louder than my thoughts. I wanted to just yell, but who would hear me? Poetry was my way of letting others who were suffering as I knowing that no matter that God requests what you have or don't have, you need to press on.I had twelve weak evil spirits inside. Now my confidential blood lamb runs victory daily.

My book helped me afraid, trembled, and annoyed and fearless reassurance lifted my spirits. Helpful are firm and worthy goals, beliefs and wishes those achievement wet and day seasons. Moreover, I wanted realize some times if I answerability the reasons for mistakes. I do inner pain is inside my book and reading over all over again. My poetry is about my journey within and the empowerment I received, by taking my healing out of man's hand and trusting God for my total healing. What you are about to read is my story, and through it I hope you will accept that there is only one creator. And his spirit and energy lives within us all.